Recipes for a Nervous Breakdow
n

GILL BOOKS

RECIPES

FOR A

NERVOUS

BREAKDOWN*

SOPHIE

WHITE

*AND HOW TO
COOK YOURSELF SANE(ISH)

Dublin 12
www.gillbooks.ie

Gill Books is an imprint of M.H. Gill & Co.

© Sophie White 2016

978 07171 7090 6

Designed by www.grahamthew.com
Photography by Leo Byrne
Food and props styled by Jette Verdi
Edited by Fiona Biggs
Indexed by Eileen O'Neill
Printed by BZ Graf, Poland

Props
Article: www.articledublin.com
Industry & Co: www.industryandco.com
Scout: scoutdublin.com

This book is typeset in 11 on 15pt Monotype Baskerville.

The paper used in this book comes from the wood pulp of
managed forests. For every tree felled, at least one tree is planted,
thereby renewing natural resources.

A CIP catalogue record for this book is available from the British
Library.

5 4 3 2 1

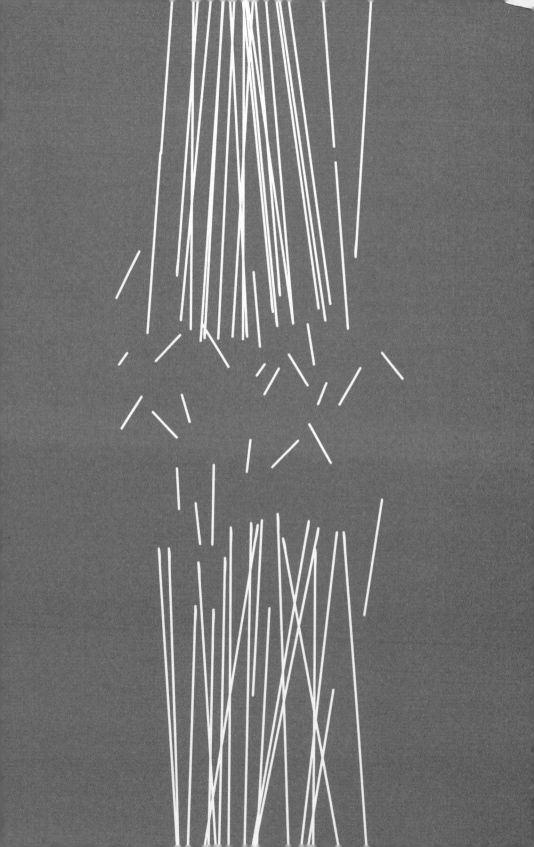

Contents

Dedication

To Roo, who made my life,
and Bugg, whom I can't
wait to meet.

Introduction

Earlier this year I was out one night trying desperately to extract myself from another round. I was making noises about leaving and my companions were doing that uniquely Irish thing of refusing to let me go. They kept saying, 'It's only 12, stay, staaaaaaay. You don't have to be up till eight.' I was doing the maths of how many hours sleep I'd be able to squeeze in if I stayed for one more hour, then got up with the baby during the night, say twice, and then skipped the shower in the morning – I had a young baby; of course I wanted to stay!

My calculations were interrupted by a drunken friend of my pals who swayed up to me and said, 'I know you. You're the one with that column all about your perfect life, and your perfect baby.' From the way he was forcefully spitting out the word 'perfect' I deduced that he was probably not a fan. I skipped the last drink and headed home to my 'perfect' husband asleep on the couch with one hand partially submerged inside his 'perfect' chipper snackbox that was still 'perfectly' balanced on his chest. I made my way to bed only to be woken an hour later by my 'perfect' baby.

It was not an encounter that affected me too deeply, though I did find myself mulling over the 'perfect' thing for a few days.

Obviously no one's life is perfect, though (touch wood) mine is certainly pretty good. I wasn't born in Victorian times and expected to wear an apparatus restricting my human right to breathe. I have never been held hostage by a reality TV-loving maniac who forces me (using that thing from *A Clockwork Orange*, I presume) to watch every episode of the *Keeping Up with the Kardashians* ever made – though TBH I'd probably love that. I have all my limbs (currently). I love and am loved. So, my drunken friend (and, beware, this may enrage you further), you might be wrongish but you're not so far off.

It did get me thinking, however, about how misleading a weekly snapshot of one's life can be. 'The Domestic', the column I started four years ago for the *Sunday Independent*, was pitched ostensibly as a relationship column about a couple of newlyweds navigating the choppy waters of domestic bliss, with an accompanying recipe each week.

People who enjoyed the column and tuned in regularly to keep up to date with Himself's weight or Herself's attachment issues told me they liked its honesty. Once a woman emailed me and thanked me for writing about how I didn't like my baby son all that much when he was first born (in case he's reading, I'm paraphrasing somewhat). She said it had made her feel better.

Obviously this is exactly the kind of function I want my writing to serve. I would like people to feel better about their lives after reading about mine. And I want people to be amused and I want people to be nourished (hence the recipes). When Gill Books approached me about creating a book with 'The Domestic' I wasn't sure where to begin. It seemed impossible to write a cookbook that has so much rambling biography in it while still retaining its cookbookyness, yet the idea of divorcing the recipes from the anecdotes left me cold.

As I read through old columns it struck me that as much as I put out there from my life, as with everyone's lives there was a wider narrative that I had never really touched on because it wasn't quite the place for it. I had a breakdown in my early 20s, spent the next few years trying to recover from it and, in quite a circuitous fashion, I wound up cooking for a living. *Recipes for a Nervous Breakdown* is not a how-to for navigating psychosis or your 20s or even surviving your mother, it's just an accumulation of those years spent trying to piece myself together after going mad. It's not written from a place of any kind of enlightenment; I am not finished getting better, as my most recent foray into madness illustrates. But it is written from a place of having gotten on with things.

I wanted to write about my experience because I felt it might be something that would have benefitted me to read back then. It's not a promise of being fixed. I suppose I just wanted to say that all the crap things in life can become incidentals rather than the point. For a good five years or so I felt very defined by the medication I had been prescribed and by the diagnosis I was given (some form of drug-induced episode). I fully and utterly believed that I was broken for good, and maybe I am. But so are we all. *Recipes for a Nervous Breakdown* is for laughing at the silly stuff, crying about some sad things, each staring down our own personal madness and eating some delicious food while we're at it.

CHAPTER 1

Poof and you're pɐɯ

In which I ATTEMPT TO EXPLAIN what this book is about.

BEFORE GOING MAD, I DIDN'T REALLY GIVE MADNESS THAT MUCH THOUGHT. IT seemed like a distant concept that had absolutely zero bearing on my life. A life that had been pretty average up until that point. I was born in 1985 in Dublin's Rotunda Hospital, the first and only child of Kevin and Mary (aka Herself). So far, so good.

I grew up. I went to school. I played with my friends. I watched *Bosco, Zig and Zag, Blossom, Saved by the Bell, Party of Five*. I loved drawing and making things. I loved reading and telling stories. Up and up I grew. I played Mrs Bennet in 5th Class. I went to secondary school. I wore black, I listened to Green Day. I did reasonably well in exams. I still loved art and started to do photography. I had a small group of really close friends. I kissed boys. I was fat but not as fat as I thought I was. I wasn't pretty but I wasn't as ugly as I thought I was. I wanted to be an artist.

I grew up and up. I did my Leaving Cert and went to art college. I drank wine and smoked. I did drugs. I made sculptures. I hugged a tree the first time I ever did magic mushrooms and cried because the stars were so pretty. I worked in a restaurant. I worked at the dogs. I was heartbroken and I fell in love. I lay on a blanket under a tree in the garden and loved a new boy. I went to parties. I read books and drew pictures. I wrote my thesis and ate takeaways. I drank too much and got sick. I had a bathtub beside my bed and lay reading in the water.

I got my first at college and worked in a bookshop. I wondered what to do next.

I bought a plane ticket but ended up missing the flight. I was going along, living the life that I knew.

I thought going mad was a gradual kind of state – after all that's what the phrase kind of suggests. But for me it was an instantaneous transformation. Poof and you're mad. Most people have watershed moments in life, the events that divide the life they had from the new reality, and this was mine. Electric Picnic, Saturday 1 September 2007. Wake up one morning in a field with your friends with no idea that by the next morning everything will be changed irrevocably. Poof and you're mad.

Funnily enough, the moment when my life made this cataclysmic shift actually felt physically like a shift. I had taken a pill about an hour earlier and was walking through a field when I felt the familiar unbearable lightness of coming up on Ecstasy. Then I felt an unmistakable jolt, like an abrupt jerk in the Earth's orbit. I was unnerved but shook it off. I'd had the odd bad trip before on mushrooms and knew that entertaining the seeds of doubt can virtually bring on the badness, but if you brush them off and focus on positives sometimes you can essentially style it out.

If all this is making me sound like a seasoned druggie, believe me, I was not. To my mind I was very moderate in my drug taking. Though with hindsight my frame of reference might have been a bit skewed as I had just come through art college, where the attitudes were possibly a bit more lenient than your average campus.

Anyway, back to the 'Poof and you're mad' bit. I soon realised that I would not be shrugging off this bad trip. It was taking complete hold of me by the time I managed to make my way back to my tent. A bad trip is different for everyone, but the gist is this: extreme anguish, profound terror, with or without auditory and visual hallucinations. Fun.

I lay in that tent for hours and hours, racked with terror. On many levels I thought I was going to die and had full-blown hallucinations of talking to my parents about this. But somewhere I had an element of conscious awareness. I felt I would survive. I just needed to rehydrate! I had a few litres of water in the tent with me, and as I rode each wave of anxiety and blackest fear I clung to this one act of trying to cleanse myself of the drug and get to morning. At some point near dawn I fell asleep.

Upon waking I initially felt profound relief. I had survived the night, the drug was wearing off and we were heading home. I still had the uneasy feary feeling of a bad, bad hangover, but I was glad to be out of that tent. I distinctly remember thinking that I would never take drugs again. What I didn't realise then was that I would be reliving elements of that first night over and over for the next few years. That it would be four years before I would feel stable enough to have even a glass of wine with dinner and that I would wind up on drugs of a very different variety.

The first few days after the trip I noticed that the persistent fear and anxiety were showing no signs of abating and appeared to be getting worse. I was also having strange visual and auditory disturbances. I found watching television absolutely unbearable, as the onslaught of sounds and images felt like an attack on my frazzled brain. Trips to the supermarket or other crowded places were such an aggressive assault on my senses that I avoided them at all costs. I had begun to notice that everyday objects looked unfamiliar to me. This is hard to describe, but completely innocuous things like shampoo bottles and boxes of cereal would appear altered and fill me with dread. Even my own face and hands were frightening to me.

One night as I was washing dishes my left arm suddenly felt like it was not my own. I stopped what I was doing and touched it with my other arm. I could feel it, but I couldn't shake the sense that this arm was alien and not really a part of me. I pretended to continue with the dishes while carefully watching the arm out of the corner of my eye. It too continued washing the dishes. The strangest thing was not the mistrust of my own arm but that some part of my mind could still recognise that these were not normal thoughts. I began to be plagued by the sensation that I was going mad.

During this time I experienced a lot of obsessive thoughts. The thoughts felt to me as if they were uncontrollable, that they were not my own, and I was terrified of the images that would flash across my brain. All the while I still had a scrap of rational perspective that I tried to use to talk myself down. A recurring obsessive thought was that I would kill my boyfriend. I knew without a doubt that I didn't want to kill him but I was afraid that this was where all this madness was heading. That I would wake up out of this nightmare having murdered him, pleading insanity in some highly publicised murder trial. I tried to explain these thoughts to him, and credit to him he laughed and said he could easily take me.

Weeks and weeks had passed since the Poof night and I was rapidly getting worse and worse. I was plagued by a strange physical sensation that I called 'brain nausea'. It was like a constant terror that increased and decreased in waves at all times. Another quirk of my madness had also developed. When I opened my eyes and looked around me it felt as if I was looking at things through the wrong end of a telescope. People and objects seemed very small and far away. And unreal. The unreal feeling became more and more persistent. I became quite convinced that my memory of my life was false and that nothing in this world was real. At more lucid times I tried to reason myself out of this line of thinking. I would play the Beatles and say to myself, 'If nothing is real, then does this mean you wrote this song? That you created all the art in the world and masterminded the garlic press?' Of course this was not really something I or anyone else could reason me out of. Something had been profoundly altered in my brain and there was no easy fix.

I was absolutely obsessed with pretending that everything was okay. I told none of my friends what was happening to me and I think I put up a decent enough show of normality when I had to. Pretending that I was fine did help me to feel marginally more normal when I was with them. I began to hint to my mother that I was feeling a bit off, not really myself, and she started to push for me to 'see someone'. The person closest to knowing the full extent of things was Himself. We lived together at the time in a crumbling old coach house at the bottom of his dad's garden. We had met a year before and become completely besotted with one another, so much so that in his family, we were known as 'the twins'.

Himself is a calm sort of person, which perhaps helped him to deal with what was happening to us. I also believe that I didn't ever tell him the full extent of things. I didn't tell him about the stranger's arm, or how I was afraid of my own face or the whispering in my ears. He told me later that the scariest thing was a particular look that would come over me. I would stare for long periods quite fixedly, at nothing that he could perceive, with an expression of abject terror. He would try to talk to me to break the spell and eventually I would snap back and acknowledge him. For the most part he tried to act normal and mind me. I continued to go to my job in the bookshop, though I had developed a certain paranoia relating to the place, and pretending to be fine all day in a retail environment was challenging. Completely sane people would go mad from it.

I was resisting the 'seeing someone' because I was terrified of what they would say. My mother had made a few appointments for me that I had cancelled at the last minute. I was terrified of telling anyone about my obsessive thoughts and brain sickness. I was pretty much terrified of everything. I had started my own regime of restricted diet and herbal remedies in a bid to cure myself. I was petrified of sugar, alcohol and caffeine, anything that would cause physical stimulus and exacerbate my anxiety. I was completely convinced that manuka honey and valerian would cure me.

Every night I went to bed and slept, which was a miracle, since all day every day I was plagued by my thoughts. I think that the fact that I could sleep was down to sheer exhaustion from pretending to be fine all the time. A strange thing I noticed was that in my dreams I felt normal again, and for a couple of seconds in the morning, before the rushing terror and flat unreality returned, I would think it had all gone away. It was like my worlds had reversed. The all-pervading atmosphere of dread usually felt in nightmares had become my waking reality, while when I slept I was peaceful. In my dreams was the only time I felt like myself again.

Two things happened that eventually convinced me to see a psychiatrist. First, I started to plan my suicide and, second, I met a man who had experienced what was happening to me. Not to dwell on the suicide plan, but here's a quick rundown: I was very sad about what I felt had become the inevitable outcome to all this. I had had my fun and done drugs and was now getting what was coming to me. The main emotion I felt was sadness for the people who loved me, though there was also a kind of inevitability about the whole thing, as though my life had been heading towards this conclusion all along. I had a feeling of determined resignation. I made the actual plan when I was lying beside Himself in bed one night. And I distinctly remember feeling very sorry for him and thinking, 'You poor thing, you fell in love with the wrong person'. Making the plan gave me a bleak kind of hope, a sense that this would all be over soon and I wouldn't have to feel like this any more.

How I met Andrew was pure coincidence. It seemed so very serendipitous that for quite a while I suspected that in my state of madness I was hallucinating him. I was leaving the bookshop and Andrew applied for my job. He was hired and came to work with me for two weeks so that I could show him the ropes. On the first morning he made a pot of coffee, and when I said that I didn't drink coffee any more he asked me why, and quite out of the blue I told him absolutely everything. Confiding in a complete stranger was bizarre on some level but perhaps it made a skewed kind of sense. He was a stranger who wouldn't cry or get angry or sedate me if I explained about being afraid I would kill someone or how I was planning to kill myself.

Incredibly, Andrew had been through a similar episode, also induced by drugs. He is an insanely (pardon the pun) serene person and he said a lot of things that I could hardly believe had happened to him. He had gone through psychiatrists and counsellors and seemed to be ambivalent towards psychiatric medication, but he said that he tried not to obsess too much over the meds he was prescribed. He believed it was likely they had contributed to his recovery, along with cognitive behavioural therapy and time.

In November, three months after the Poof night, I finally got the bus to St John of Gods and met my psychiatrist for the first time. I pretty much felt like I was hanging on by a thread by this time. I'm not sure if it is a common thing for a person to hate their psychiatrist, but I hated her from the first moment we met. I told her a lot of what I had been going through but held back about the obsessive thoughts and lied when she asked if I was suicidal. She gave me a prescription on my first visit for an anti-depressant called Lexapro but I didn't take it. I also began seeing a counsellor in the same clinic, who I grudgingly warmed to slightly more than the psychiatrist, mainly because, as a counsellor, he wasn't giving me prescriptions.

Still, for the first few visits I was ridiculously guarded with them both, completely defeating the purpose of our sessions. I was deeply suspicious that the psychiatrist was secretly hypnotising me, which sounded so incredibly paranoid that I was afraid to voice these concerns to the counsellor. Eventually I was prescribed and agreed to take Olanzapine ('to help with your thoughts') and the original Lexapro prescription.

Olanzapine is a type of anti-psychotic. Now, I can tell you it is pretty demoralising being prescribed an anti-psychotic. The anti-depressant prescription confused me as I didn't imagine that what I was suffering from was depression, but the anti-psychotic seemed to confirm my worst fears. Poof and you're mad.

Anyone who has ever been on Olanzapine can probably attest to the fact that it is officially the least fun drug ever. The feeling Olanzapine gives you is sedation without contentment. It helped with my thoughts on some level, in that while I was on it I was hardly able to make eye contact, never mind form coherent thoughts. Every night I took my Olanzapine at 8.00 pm and by 8.15 I was barely capable of speech. The first few nights I took it I didn't anticipate the effect it would have on my co-ordination and found I was hardly able to use a knife and fork.

One evening Himself and I went to dinner with all our parents. It was an awkward meal. I was, as usual, making an exhausted and largely unsuccessful effort to appear fine. The reservation was for 7.30 pm and I was besieged with panic from the moment we sat down.

At the time I hated being in any scenario that required me to sit still for any period of time. Car rides were excruciating and I was phobic about public transport as I felt trapped. On trains, I was fixated on the fact that if I needed to bail out at a moment's notice I was at the mercy of automated doors.

In the restaurant we were seated at a large round table in quite a plush dining room. On the wall across from the table was a large mirror framed in padded leather. This is where my studied calm began to unravel. As we were taking our seats I caught sight of my reflection with my peripheral vision and a thought came unbidden to me. There were always a lot of disjointed thoughts assaulting me at any given time but this one made me feel sick to my stomach, which, in a bizarre kind of way, seemed immediately to lend this thought more credence. It stood out from the rest of the cacophony because it had produced a physical reaction. The stand-out thought was: 'There's the other me, the real me.'

I don't know if everyone with drug-induced psychosis has these fixations on doubles, but I certainly had. I frequently harboured suspicions that those around me were in fact replacements, like pod people, in the same way that I felt that I, myself, had been replaced.

Throughout the meal I tried not to look at the mirror but I was deeply unnerved by any glimpse of my reflection, or, as I saw it, *her* presence. My grasp on the situation was tenuous. The parents were chatting away, apparently unaware, as I tried to focus on acting fine. Fine, fine, fine. My hands were always shaky and my mouth was always dry from the medication, but around this time each night, as 8.00 pm and my nightly dose approached, I always felt that the incessant thoughts and dread that ebbed and flowed all day would start to hit a crescendo until I took the pill, when all would go quiet and I would become slack.

At this dinner I tried to hold out on taking the Olanzapine – after all, a tense and watchful person is still preferable to a person verging on catatonia unable to piece a sentence together, especially at a dinner party. In the end, though, the crescendo was peaking and I made my way to the bathroom and took my pill. Soon after, Himself made some excuse and took me home before the main course. Presumably the parents glossed over my behaviour and got on with getting along. It was the first time they had all met.

The Olanzapine admittedly did provide some relief from the fractured and relentless thoughts that tormented me and caused frequent shocks of cold fear in my chest. And the feelings of unreality seemed distant and less threatening under the cloak of sedation. The feeling induced by the medication was that someone had thrown a thick felt blanket over all these sensations. I could still feel them through the material but they were blunted by the meds. They didn't seem so vivid or relevant to me anymore. Then again, nothing in my life seemed vivid or relevant anymore. I sat on the edge of my bed and idly wondered where I had gone, while also noting how odd it was that, it seemed, I no longer cared.

PEANUT BUTTER CUPS

I am absolutely nuts about peanut butter (I am also an unashamed punner). I thought what better recipe to kick off a genre-melding cookbook-memoir hybrid about someone going nuts than a recipe containing nuts?

I was first introduced to Reese's Peanut Butter Cups by the impossibly cool American cousins back in 1993 on a trip to the States with my parents. The American cousins called sweets 'candy' and footpath 'sidewalk', and they were in junior high as opposed to Our Lady of Mercy National School. Fuck, they were cool.

As you will see, I am a little bit obsessed with making my own versions of popular confectionery items as it usually gives the items a deeper, more complex flavour. And I am a bit fanatical about chocolate to filling ratio. In my book no one gets this right except me. **Makes 12**

- 300g plain chocolate
- 80g stoned dates
- 3 tablespoons smooth peanut butter
- 1 tablespoon coconut oil
- 2 tablespoons ground almonds
- 1–2 tablespoons almond milk

You will need:
- 12 paper cupcake cases

Put the chocolate into a heatproof bowl set over a saucepan of barely simmering water. Heat, stirring frequently, until melted. Remove from the heat and leave to stand for a couple of minutes.

Using a teaspoon, carefully line the paper cases with the melted chocolate, drawing the chocolate about 2cm up the sides of the cases, then place them in the freezer to set. Keep the remaining melted chocolate warm to use later.

Put the dates, peanut butter, oil and almonds into a food processor and blend to a smooth paste. Add the almond milk, a little at a time, to achieve a soft consistency.

When the chocolate moulds are set, fill each one with the date mixture – it's quite sticky, so use the back of a damp teaspoon to smooth the filling. Seal the top of each chocolate with a teaspoon of melted chocolate.

Return the peanut butter cups to the freezer until set completely.

WHITE CHOCOLATE AND PEANUT BUTTER FUDGE

Continuing on the nut theme, I made this peanut butter fudge for the first time last Mother's Day, when I cleverly concocted a plan to call in sick to life and stayed in bed watching back-to-back movie trailers in a state of relaxation bordering on catatonia. That was a good day. **Makes 30 pieces**

- oil or butter, for greasing
- 300g white chocolate chips
- 400ml tinned condensed milk
- 300g smooth peanut butter
- 75g chopped salted cashew nuts

Line a 21cm square baking tray with baking paper. Lightly grease the paper with a little oil or butter. Put the chocolate chips, condensed milk and peanut butter into a heavy-based saucepan set over a low heat. Stir until melted and thoroughly combined.

When the mixture is smooth, add the cashew nuts to the pan and stir them through. Pour the fudge mixture evenly into the prepared tray. Smooth the top of the fudge.

Place in the fridge for about 1 hour to speed up the setting process.

When the fudge is firm, turn it out onto a board and carefully peel off the paper. Cut into 30 bite-sized pieces and store in an airtight container in the fridge.

PEANUT-DRESSED ASIAN-STYLE CHICKEN SALAD

The peanut butter obsession knows no bounds. Himself indulges in a bi-weekly gripe about the hipster takeover that is peanut butter's rise to foodie favour. I try to explain to him that on paper, at least, we too are hipsters; between us we've got facial hair, asymmetrical haircuts, niche taste in condiments and the odd tattoo, but he is in deep denial on this one. So much so that I often lie to him about peanut butter inclusions to avoid a hypocritical rant. This salad dressing is so tasty it will seduce even the most salad-resistant peeps (I'm talking about Himself, obviously). **Serves 2**

- *2 teaspoons crunchy peanut butter*
- *2 teaspoons dark miso paste*
- *juice of ½ lime*
- *3 tablespoons water*
- *1 teaspoon soft brown sugar*
- *½ red chilli, deseeded and finely diced*
- *1 carrot, cut into matchsticks*
- *1 red pepper, deseeded and thinly sliced*
- *2 spring onions, sliced*
- *1 head of baby gem lettuce, roughly shredded*
- *40g mixed fresh basil, mint and coriander, finely chopped*
- *2 cooked chicken breasts, roughly torn*
- *60g roasted cashew nuts*

Put the peanut butter, miso paste, lime juice, water, sugar and chilli into a large bowl and whisk until well combined.

Add the carrot, red pepper, spring onions, lettuce, herbs and chicken to the dressing and toss well until all the components are evenly coated. Divide the mixture between two bowls and scatter the roasted cashew nuts over the top.

CHAPTER 2

Going through with

In which I have the strong urge to skip my own wedding, and reflect on my time LIVING IN A VAN in rural France eating baked goods and railing against certain INFURIATING ASPECTS of the French mentality.

ON THE EVE OF MY WEDDING I WAS PRETTY SURE THAT I WOULDN'T BE GETTING married. Himself and I had spent the late afternoon in wellies, decorating a flooded tent with home-made bunting, while water levels slowly rose over our toes and eventually to ankle height. We were resolutely not mentioning the weather – it was 7 June 2012 and flood warnings had been issued in the east, west and south of the country. The other thing that we were not talking about was the fact that I was still uncertain as to whether I would indeed be attending this party – a fact Himself was possibly unaware of.

We said goodbye and I made my way back to Sandymount where I was spending my final maiden night at my mother's house, as per the custom. I was feeling increasingly wild and desperate as I cycled into sideways rain in Ballsbridge. The minutes were ticking past. I was definitely not going to do this, I decided.

Making this decision calmed me somewhat, though I had no clear idea exactly how I wouldn't be going through with it. For some reason the ferry to Holyhead is the escape route that always presents itself during the many times I have plotted my exit. Silly, as there are so many better options available now. I think it is a hangover from my youth when air travel posed too much of a logistical headache to my 12-year-old self to be a realistic plan. My life in Holyhead would be made up of simple days. I'd reinvent myself as a plucky bartender or waitress, perhaps take up macramé. Sure, I'd miss Himself and Herself and my friends, but it was the price I was willing to pay at that point just to get out of getting married.

I'd like to say that this was an isolated incident of complete mania, but actually this is my natural knee-jerk reaction to virtually every good thing that has ever happened in my life. I have a complete inability to plan anything and comfortably go through with it. Committing to lunch plans more than 12 hours in advance is a struggle for me. Good luck to anyone who tries to get a firm answer out of me on some long-range plan. It's not going to happen.

Before Himself actually proposed to me I was pretty certain that I wanted to marry him. We had been going out for years. I liked him. There were no major defects like those I had perceived in previous boyfriends. Most of what could be considered character flaws were things that only made me more attracted to him – his arrogance, for one. In his own eyes, Himself is the single greatest living specimen of the human male. As far as he is concerned, he is the pinnacle, the apex of perfection of this species. His only true flaw, as far as he will admit, is his infuriating habit of song-jacking. This is when one person is happily singing a song as they go about their day and another person cuts across them and proceeds to sing a new song more loudly, thus drowning out the original song. Song-jacking. It's infuriating.

So when the proposal came I answered, without hesitation, 'Yes!' I was 26 years old and hadn't showered in days. We were in a campsite in western France, in a town called Ribeauvillé. The town is in a region known as the mini-Alps and we had been doing a lot of cycling in the area. We were living at the time in a van that we had bought sight unseen off the Internet. Remember, this was 2011, the days before people routinely bought designer handbags and wives sight unseen off the Internet. For our friends and family the purchase of the van seemed to cement their idea of us as borderline vagrants unlikely to achieve much in life. And the manner in which we had purchased the van did nothing to help our image. In the halcyon early days of the van we lived on the edge of an idyllic car park high in the French Alps, stealing electricity from the local commune municipale and washing down copious pains au raisins with competitively priced petrol wine. La vie en rose.

By the time the proposal came we had taken to the road in the van, pushing the boundaries of what the van was capable of – nothing over 40 miles an hour, apparently. Luckily, we had no jobs to speak of, having saved money working the winter in the Alps, nor any pressing engagements, so pulling over any time the van overheated or started to emit a noxious smell was totally fine. The main focus of each day was leisurely perusing the aisles of whatever hypermarché we happened to pass.

Browsing French supermarkets is the single most enjoyable aspect of living in France. This and the petrol wine. At all other times living in France can be a draining experience and one that has left me with an underlying, simmering rage towards the French as a nation. Life in France as a non-national tends to lurch from one bureaucratic headache to the next – this is a country where one requires a permit just to own a goldfish. We constantly found ourselves trapped in petty administrative catch-22s, whereby we would need to do something basic like rent somewhere to live but had to produce documentation of our current residence in order to do so. 'If we had a current residence than we wouldn't need this residence!' I would eventually shriek in perfect French, to which they would respond in English that was considerably harder to understand than my French efforts.

The language barrier is a further extension of my animosity towards the French. I always get the distinct impression that they are deliberately not understanding our attempts to speak their language. 'Bonjour!' we say and they respond with a determinedly baffled expression. 'You know what I said!' I once screamed with completely disproportionate anger. It was a cumulative rage build-up from being on the receiving end of French attitude for years at that stage.

Anyway, whatever about the people, I adore a French supermarket. I enjoy a place where you can buy wine by the bottle, box and bag while also purchasing some budget underwear and a commercial-grade water pump – all essentials that are stocked side by side in every good supermarket. The average French supermarket also devotes at least 20 per cent of its floor space to the yogurt aisle. The French adore their yogurts and the yogurt aisle is where they go to worship.

As we lived in a van with no method of refrigeration more sophisticated than storing goods next to cold cans under the bed we had a healthy disregard for sell-by dates and storage instructions. We were fortunate to be living in a country that has a high regard for goods that can be stored at room temperature and appear to be all but impervious to the passage of time. Most visitors from Ireland and the UK complain about the creepy long-life milk favoured by the French, but we embraced it, as it could withstand the climate of the van. Also, the long-life milk, for us, was actually a step up from the powdered milk that we lived on the summer before when we were living in a tent and bicycles were our only mode of transport. During that summer, in a strange act of masochistic economy, we used powdered milk in our tea and on our cereal as it was long-lasting and more practical to transport by bike than the indulgent 'liquid' milk.

The year of the van we developed a focused and highly considered weekly menu that was sensitive to our storage limitations. I also adopted a comprehensive outline of which sell-by dates to ignore and which to abide by. The first day of the weekly shop was chicken day (as not even I was cavalier enough to fuck with chicken), the next day was fish day. Wild, right? Not really, as we'd buy it frozen and allow it to thaw overnight. Genius. That is, unfortunately, where my ingenuity ran

out, and the rest of the week would be dominated by meals of canned origin, punctuated by the few foods I deemed hardy enough to roll on into next week; sausages (because of their high fat content), cured meats and saucisson (already preserved), packets of pre-grated Emmenthal cheese (so synthetic that it bore little resemblance to actual food), eggs (are supposed to be stored at room temperature in any event; pet peeve 001: people who keep eggs in the fridge) and hardy vegetables.

While living in France, we mostly ate merguez sausages – a skinny, dark, spicy sausage that everyone must become acquainted with as soon as possible if not earlier – and baguette soaked in the drippings of merguez sausages. Living in a van means that cleaning the dishes can be a bit of a faff. Luckily Himself always obliged in so far as he would basically scrub the dishes with the crusty outer side of the baguettes, then soak up the dripping with the spongy absorbent bread side, which he would then devour in a highly economical dish-cleaning method that required no water and produced no waste.

In the days leading up to the proposal, Himself had been acting shifty, though I didn't think much of it at the time. Most days we would leave the van and, armed with water, a map (so quaint) and a large supply of pain au chocolat, we would strike out on the bikes to conquer a nearby col. Later he told me that he had been intending to propose to me on one of these bike rides.

I really do wonder about men sometimes. What woman wants to be proposed to while sweating profusely and wearing Lycra? By a man whose penis silhouette is most unfortunately visible through his own Lycra? Not to mention that I was sporting an unfortunate version of tarring and feathering that involved sun cream and insects. And being proposed to by a man whose beard is similarly caked in sun block with the remnants of a hastily demolished pain au chocolat adhering to his face? With a few hundred tourists milling around? These spots were always a favourite with bus tours as the views are stunning.

Luckily, Himself was struggling to get the words out. We would reach the top of whatever arduous route we were doing and he would just kind of stare helplessly at me. At the time I put it down to his lack of fitness – he's always been weaker on the climbs – but apparently he was just trying to marshal his resolve. It probably didn't help that I would immediately go in search of the nearest ice cream vendor and had no idea that I was messing with his proposal scheme.

In the end I think the pressure got to him, which is why he just blurted the words out one night after dinner, in the same sentence as an inquiry as to the whereabouts of the Fairy Liquid. I was lying in the hammock we'd tied between the van and a tree reading my book when he jumped in beside me. I remember feeling very irked, as he is enormous and immediately squished me. I think 'hammock-jacking' may, in that moment, have been added to 'song-jacking' in my mental tally of his flaws. 'Where's the Fairy Liquid … and will you marry me?'

As I said previously, I answered without a thought to what I was setting in motion. I laughed. He cried. And for the first couple of hours we were delighted with ourselves.

Getting engaged in a random town where you know no one is a slightly bizarre experience. We took ourselves off to the local town square in search of a pay phone. I suppose the first inkling of mania could have been detected when I suggested that we just tell our parents for the time being and wait to let it 'bed in' before telling any of our friends. Himself was willing to humour me at this point and agreed.

We phoned our parents to deliver the news, which was met with varying degrees of amusement and bemusement. I think they were too polite to say that as borderline vagrants who lived in a van and subsisted on sausages we really had no business getting married. I also imagine that they thought we were too young, but nay-saying someone's proposal, especially over a pay phone, was probably a conversation Herself just didn't have the energy for at that moment.

Instead she just said 'Really?' several times, before handing the phone to my father, who laughed and laughed.

A passing American tourist had happened to catch the gist of our conversation and presently invited us for a celebratory drink. We joined her outside a café on the square and toasted our proposal. I didn't really drink at the time and concentrated on pretend-sipping my champagne, and at some point discreetly swapped my full glass for Himself's empty one.

The American was a lively woman called Debra who lived in Berne, Switzerland, and had once licked Colin Farrell for a dare in a bar. She was palling around Ribeauvillé with a young guy whose connection to her we couldn't quite make out, but who also seemed to be on the receiving end of her generosity. We were offered a honeymoon in Berne should we so wish, and at the end of our encounter she pressed her business card on me and said she would always be the woman who bought us a drink on the day of our engagement, which is indeed true.

A few days passed and the 'bedding in' period was spent hunting for an engagement ring and bickering about when was a good time to tell the rest of our friends. 'Never' was becoming the all-dominating thought circling around my head. I began to feel extremely anxious any time I thought of the engagement or whenever Himself wanted to talk about it, which was often. He would muse on what kind of wedding to have and when to have it, with the expected enthusiasm of any newly engaged, rational person. He was excited to take the next step in life, while I couldn't sleep at night because of panicking that we shouldn't get married.

I had never questioned our relationship before this but, suddenly, when faced with the oppressive spectre of marriage, I became convinced that we shouldn't get married. I spent the next week in a state of unhinged panic. What if we changed and started to hate each other? What if he wasn't right for me or if I went mad and killed him in his sleep? 'Why did I say yes?', I would lament to Himself, lounging in the passenger seat, bare feet pressed up against the windscreen while he drove us through tiny French towns with ramshackle stone châteaux and a dog by the fountain in the centre of every square. 'If we get married everything will change, and we'll end up hating each other.' Himself seemed utterly unconcerned about my backtracking. I whinged and angled to get out of it, but he refused to entertain any of this. I'd said yes and he was holding me to it.

Eventually it was Herself who talked me down and convinced me to go with it. After seven sleepless nights and much pleading with Himself I rang my mother and unloaded a week's worth of anxiety-driven totally irrational thoughts on her in one fell swoop.

She tried to reassure me that I couldn't be certain that any of my predicted horrible outcomes would actually happen. In any case, she reasoned, if they did come to pass, there was always divorce or, in the case of the spousal homicide, she would generously provide me with an alibi. This is information that I may one day regret committing to print as it could be used in the prosecution case against me if I do end up murdering Himself, though in that event this whole book could potentially be damning evidence.

After I recited my litany of fears down the phone to her, she asked in a low, concerned voice: 'Have you said any of this to him?' 'Oh yeah,' I responded. 'He's right here beside me.'

She told me then and there that I had better marry him, as no other person in the world would sit there and listen to this level of neurosis just days after getting engaged and not run away very quickly indeed.

A year later and now the wedding was less than 24 hours away. Himself had planned the entire thing with the kind of dogged persistence of a man who knew that the biggest challenge of this wedding would not be the price of floral arrangements or the considerable pitfalls of bringing together many branches of an estranged family, but rather just ensuring that his soon-to-be wife would attend.

I helped out on the more fun aspects of organising the event – buying a wedding dress and making decorations – but any time there were more tiresome details to be worked out I would fade away like a Victorian lady with her smelling salts and feign a kind of lethargic hysteria. The engagement anxiety would overcome me and suddenly I'd be too 'stressed' to get a quote for a generator. Looking back, Himself must've really wanted to marry me, or else just really didn't want to lose months of planning. Either way, there I was looking east to the bright lights of Holyhead and wondering whether one could feasibly stand somebody up at the altar but still go to the afters?

SAVOURY CRÊPES

Crêpes were a major favourite during the van era. We were perpetually broke and always longing to go for a menu du jour in the endless inviting restaurants we passed. I love the French thing of a three-course meal in the middle of the day, though as I usually need a post-lunch nap after a bowl of soup and a sandwich, somehow I don't think I have the constitution for regular menus du jour.

I believe that we are all entitled to irrationally hate one nationality, a kind of a xenophobic 'get out of jail free' card, and for years I had reserved mine for the Australians (so tanned, so confident, so annoying), but since residing in France (in a van with a British registration), I transferred my intolerance to our Gallic neighbours, as most of my interactions usually resulted in rapidly escalating screaming matches. Such is the frustrating and bureaucratic nature of living in France.

Though, love them or hate them, I have just this to say about the French: crêpes, pain au chocolat, cheese, Gauloises, Simone de Beauvoir, lime-flavoured Doritos, Rodin, fondue. Respect. They're talented – who cares if they're rude? They've earned it.

Makes a lovely light summer supper when served with salad. **Serves 2 (6 crêpes)**

- 150g plain flour
- ½ teaspoon salt
- 1 egg
- 270ml milk
- 30g melted butter
- rapeseed oil, for frying
- filling of your choice
- leafy green salad, to serve

Filling suggestions:
- ham, Gruyère cheese, fresh parsley
  and mushrooms
- Parma ham, fresh figs and
  Parmesan cheese
- smoked salmon, avocado and lemon
  mascarpone, with chopped chives

Preheat the oven to 180°C/Gas 4. Place the flour and salt in a large bowl. Put the egg and milk into a separate bowl and whisk until well combined.

Make a well in the centre of the flour and gradually whisk in the egg and milk mixture until you have a smooth batter with no lumps of flour. Whisk in the melted butter.

Lightly oil a crêpe pan or small non-stick frying pan and place over a high heat. Speed is key when frying crêpes, as is accepting that you will most likely mess up the first one.

When the pan is hot, pour in about a ladleful of batter, then quickly tilt the pan to spread the batter evenly and thinly over the base. Cook for about 2 minutes on one side until little bubbles form around the edge and then, using a spatula, flip the crêpe and cook for a further 1 minute.

Remove from the pan. Lightly wipe the pan with kitchen paper and add a little more oil before cooking the next crêpe. Repeat until you have used all the batter.

Arrange the crêpes on baking trays. Cover half of each crêpe with the filling of your choice and fold over. Pop the crêpes in the oven to warm through before serving with a leafy green salad.

Crêpes de la resistance!

VAN PIZZA

This bastardised pizza was a favourite during the camper van years and is so easy it doesn't even require an actual oven. To any Italians reading this, I apologise for my crimes against your culinary heritage. Just remember, the Americans have done worse over the years – Chigago deep dish, anybody? In the van I had a small camping stove with two rings and, crucially, a small grill for melting the cheese. I used to put the dough together in the mornings and then prove it on the engine of the van as we drove – yum, hygienic! **Makes 2 individual pizzas**

- *200g plain flour, plus extra for dusting*
- *1 teaspoon salt*
- *½ teaspoon dried yeast*
- *130ml lukewarm water*
- *1 tablespoon olive oil, plus extra for brushing*
- *sea salt, for sprinkling*
- *dressed salad leaves, to serve*

Topping
- *6 tablespoons tomato purée*
- *2 x 125g balls fresh mozzarella cheese, torn into pieces*
- *6 slices Parma ham*
- *handful of stoned black olives (optional)*
- *handful of sun-dried tomatoes (optional)*

Place the flour and 1 teaspoon of salt in a bowl. Put the yeast into a cup with the water and leave to stand for 5 minutes. When small bubbles appear the yeast is working. Add the oil to the yeast mixture.

Make a well in the middle of the flour and pour in the yeast mixture. Using your hands, bring the mixture together to form a ball of dough. Turn out the dough onto a surface lightly dusted with flour and knead for about 5 minutes until smooth and elastic. Clean the bowl and brush it with a little oil.

Return the dough to the bowl, cover with a tea towel and leave to prove in a warm place for about 1 hour until doubled in size – camper van engine optional! Knock back the dough, knead again for a few minutes, then cut it into two pieces. On a surface lightly dusted with flour, roll out each piece to a diameter of 20cm, brush with oil and sprinkle with a little sea salt.

Heat a frying pan and fry the pizza bases on each side for about 5 minutes until they puff up and the base is quite crisp. This bread is not very yeasty and it cooks very quickly.

Preheat the grill. Spread the pizza bases with the tomato purée and cover with the cheese, ham, olives, if using, and sun-dried tomatoes, if using.

Pop the pizzas under the preheated grill to melt the cheese. Serve with dressed leaves.

MERGUEZ SAUSAGES WITH WHITE BEANS AND HERBS

As promised, a way to get acquainted with merguez sausages in a slightly more upmarket fashion than eating them directly out of the pan in the back of a van.

Serves 2

- 6 skinny merguez sausages
- 1 tablespoon olive oil
- 1 garlic clove
- 1 teaspoon finely chopped fresh rosemary
- zest and juice of ½ lemon
- 240g tinned cannellini beans (drained weight), rinsed
- generous handful of mixed flat-leaf parsley and basil, roughly chopped

Heat a non-stick frying pan over a high heat, add the sausages and fry until golden and cooked through.

Gently heat the oil in a saucepan over a low heat, then add the garlic, rosemary and lemon zest and stir until the flavours release.

Pour in the beans and toss to coat well. Stir in the lemon juice and a little oil from the sausages and remove from the heat. Spoon the beans onto warmed plates, top with the sausages and scatter over the parsley and basil.

Drink a glass of very cold, dry white wine with this and soak up the juices with some good bread.

CHAPTER 3

Only the

lonely

In which I attempt to put everything that's wrong with my life down to being an ONLY CHILD.

OBVIOUSLY I CAN'T BLAME ABSOLUTELY EVERYTHING THAT'S EVER HAPPENED to me on my being an only child. However, after I had gained a few years' distance from my childhood I came to realise that being an only child had impacted massively on my development. After spending time in friends' homes and around their families I realised what a huge disservice was done to me by my parents' lack of continued procreating.

My mother maintains that after six fruitless years of trying – incidentally I hate that part of the story, I'm always terrified that she'll go into more detail and I'll be left with some horrific image of my parents having sex that I will never be able to un-see. The fact that it will be joining what is already a bank of real images of my parents having sex is most unfortunate, and has probably largely contributed to whatever personality defects I possess that were not caused by being an only child.

Anyway, back to all that trying – shudder – that they were doing. Nothing was happening for them despite their evident enthusiasm for the job and so they went to see a doctor who, legend has it, told them that they were both infertile. So they abandoned all hope and presumably consoled themselves in the bedroom, because one day I was born.

On the day in question, 26 March 1985, my mother woke early in the morning to find she was in labour and informed my dad. I can so easily picture their youthful enthusiasm as they made their way carefully to the hospital, transporting their hard-won miracle baby. The familiar old cliché that Herself, who wanted an all-natural birth, was soon screaming for the epidural by 11.00 am was in evidence. The tale then veers from narrative convention at this point when my father, who had previously been instructed to do so, intervened and calmly told the nurses over his anguished wife's cries that she didn't want and wouldn't be having the epidural. This was 1985, and most of the nurses had been raised on marching for the pill and shoulder pads. They sported bleached buzz cuts and looked at this vile man like he was an abuser.

I never asked my dad whether he was a feminist. But I did witness my parents' marriage, which was the most astonishingly equal partnership I can imagine. If it is actually possible to be blind to people's gender I think my dad possessed this gift. I was 30 years old by the time I thought to wonder about this and it was too late to ask him myself so I texted my mother: 'Do you think Kev was a feminist?' And was delighted when she responded, 'Absolutely. It was a fundamental part of him.' 'Did he ever refer to it?' 'Yes, often, but I can't remember any actual quote.' So there was my feminist dad being vilified by a ward full of angry nurses for respecting my mother's instructions. She got the drugs.

Telling someone while they are growing up that their very existence is actually miraculous is a dangerous style of parenting. I entered childhood society with scarily high self-esteem and a total lack of self-awareness, which would take years of casual cruelty and schoolyard bullying to break down.

One of the first inklings I got that there was a world out there that was NOT one hundred and fifty per cent about me was in Junior Infants when the teacher told us the story of Fionn Mac Cumhail and the salmon of knowledge. Now, I had already heard this story from my dad, who had told the story with myself cast as the central character, not mythical Irish legend Fionn Mac Cumhail. I did, and do to this day, suck my thumb, and Kev used the tale as a kind of origins story for how I had started sucking my thumb. His version went something like this:

> One day, when you were so young that you can't even remember these events, you were sitting by a river, fishing with a wise old man. The old man was seeking to catch the Salmon of Knowledge, a fish that was said to contain all of the world's knowledge and would bestow its great powers and wisdom on whomsoever should catch and eat this great fish. The wise old man was consumed by a desire to catch the fish and on this day he succeeded. Together you built a fire on the banks of the river and proceeded to cook the fish. At one point the old man left you in charge of the salmon while he ran to get some herbs and a lemon [slightly incongruous details were hallmarks of my father's stories]. You were given strict instructions not to eat the fish but to prevent it burning. After a few minutes you noticed part of the flesh was bubbling up and forming a blister. Without thinking you reached out and burst the blister with your thumb. The blister popped and immediately you felt a flash of pain. On impulse you stuck your thumb into your mouth to ease the burn and unwittingly consumed the tiniest fleck of the salmon's skin. The old man returned just in time to jerk your hand away from your mouth but it was too late, the spell had worked and you had already become the holder of all the world's wisdom. And that is why you suck your thumb to this day and why we called you 'Sophie', which means wisdom.

And that story is why I was an outrageous egomaniac by the time I was four. It is why I was obnoxiously superior to anyone I felt wasn't as smart as me, which was everyone – were you not listening to the

story? And why I was pretty well unanimously hated by my peers and grown-ups alike. And, finally, that story is why being an only child is the very worst thing that can happen to anyone – bar every other actually terrible thing that can happen to a person.

If I had had siblings, for starters, that story would've been wildly different. It would most likely have had a core message about sharing or being nice to your little brother or little sister. It would've been an allegory for respecting one another. It may have not been terribly effective but at least it wouldn't have created some tiny little megalomaniac who believed she was in possession of ALL the world's knowledge at the age of four. Even if the story had remained the same, had I had a sibling the outcome would have been very different. I would perhaps have basked in the glory of the tale for a few minutes after the telling. My dad would have mussed up my hair affectionately and then gone to make a cup of tea. At which point my hypothetical sibling, who had observed the scene from a shadowy vantage point just outside the hall door, would sidle in and proceed to tear me down. 'You know that story is not about you,' he/she would say, perhaps giving me a quick hair pull or arm pinch for emphasis. In that worldly way of siblings he/she would continue, 'He told *me* that story about *me* when I was going into Junior Infants too. It's not true. They don't even like you, you were adopted and then they couldn't send you back.' This is the kind of head-fucking shit that people with siblings have to deal with. It's the kind of head-fucking shit that gets them ready for the world. No child needs to be sent out into the world with an insanely inflated sense of self and openly sucking their thumb at school age. It's just begging the world to fuck with you.

Unfortunately for me, my parents were unable to produce a sibling who would keep me in check. And they, having themselves been raised in an era when parenting styles bordered on neglect, were lavish in their praise of their darling only child. They raised me to believe that I could do anything I wanted in life, which, as we all know, is quite possibly the last thing a child needs to hear. For this reason I hold them solely responsible for the great disappointment I felt when I reached the age of 25 and realised that not now, nor ever, was I going to be a star of the stage.

Even to this day, some small part of me is still incredibly shocked that I never made it as a performer, despite making absolutely no effort to pursue this dream. When I hit the age of 24 it was with deep astonishment and disappointment that I found that I wasn't a pop star and that, at this point, it was unlikely to happen as, at 24, I was at least 60 in pop star years.

It was at this juncture that I had to accept the truth: I'm just really good at party pieces. My version of DAAGBF ('Diamonds are a Girl's Best Friend') actually has some pretty awesome accompanying choreography, a routine devised by my cousin back in 1989, and I've seen no reason to amend the moves in any way. It's possible that my four-year-old self may have been better able to pull off said moves while still looking adorable than my 30-year-old self is, but when it comes to party pieces my ginormous ego usually gets the better of me and I convince myself that the grimaces visible among the audience members are grimaces of awe and adulation. Which, let's face it, they probably are.

Around this time, quite tellingly it has to be said, my favourite game was not Sylvanian Families or Lego (though they were up there), it was actually interviewing myself in the downstairs toilet of my parents' house. The toilet was located under the stairs and off the hall where presumably anybody who happened to pass by could hear the grotesque self-aggrandising dialogue from within. It is probably further testament to my narcissistic character that I made no effort to hide this self-indulgent exhibitionism and that I am now, at this point, writing this book.

What incredible achievements warranted the interview were always unclear, but one recurring theme of the interview was a bombshell I'd drop about halfway through.

Interviewer (me): 'So, Sophie, tell me, when did you know that you would become the first girl ever to portray both Elizabeth Bennett and her mother, Mrs Bennett, in a stage production of *Pride and Prejudice*? It's completely unprecedented, but the director was adamant that you were the only woman for both roles.'

Subject (me): 'Actually, Sophie's not my real name. I've never told anyone this but my name is in fact … Sharity.'

Oh yes, I was queen of the non sequitur and a fan of totally made-up names. A TV researcher's nightmare. Should I ever wind up in an interview situation I'm definitely going to drop in the old 'Sophie's not my real name' bombshell. I'll be an enigma, cloaked in intrigue and wrapped up in hair extensions.

As an only child, so many outlandish whims are indulged that it can make for a highly eccentric adult. I'd like to think I escaped this with the help of some very good friends, the Bitch Herd, who essentially demanded that I shut the fuck up any time I launched into a pretentious bullshit spiral.

For the purposes of this book I have decided to refer to the individual members of the Bitch Herd by the names we gave to each other's breasts aged 16: Siffies (that's me, so-called because my breasts are so small as to be verging on concave), Jessoms (my well-endowed pal who was lucky enough to be in possession of bona fide bosoms and knew how to use them), Fat Tits (not much explanation required here) and KaJengas, or Jenga for short (as this girl has a fairly average supply of mammary but spades of moxy, and Jenga just kind of sums her up. Also, her name is Jen.).

Jenga was the co-founder of the Bitch Herd and we met in primary school, aged four. For the next 26 years she endeavoured to save me from being mercilessly bullied and has tried to teach me how to be a person. When I met Jenga, the outward signs of only childness that I was displaying were enough to alienate me even if I did have the coolest Teenage Mutant Ninja Turtles lunchbox – which I did. I had an advanced vocabulary from socialising only with my parents and their friends. I openly sucked my thumb and twiddled my hair and the hair of unsuspecting strangers in my vicinity. I enjoyed food that other kids thought was disgusting and was so fastidious about the way my food was prepared and consumed as to be bordering on compulsive.

A typical packed lunch of my primary school era could be comprised of a pitta (toasted and cooled prior to being individually wrapped – I was OBSESSED with preventing the condensation build-up that would occur if the pitta was wrapped prematurely), Parma ham, sun-dried tomatoes, pine nuts and leaves stored in one container, and a separate portion of my mother's French dressing transported in an old film canister. The lunch would then require careful assemblage in school. I would dress and toss the salad before preparing the pitta and eating with a focus and precision that to this day I am capable of applying only to my meals. If I could channel this kind of rigorous and dedicated attention to detail into any other aspect of my life I would be very successful.

My evening meals were governed by even more rigid rules. Under no circumstances could different foodstuffs mingle on the same plate. I imposed strict segregation between all the elements of a meal. If one component of the meal was saucy it was annexed to a separate plate. Some meals required multiple plates to meet my exacting and totally inexplicable directive. None of this would be remotely remarkable were it not for the fact that this pathological behaviour continued well into my early 20s.

My meals were so protracted and drawn out that Jenga would mock me mercilessly. It wasn't unkind, she just has a low tolerance for ridiculosity and she was doing me a major solid by giving me that first clue that the rest of the world wasn't going to have a high tolerance for these foibles either.

CRISPY SALMON WITH LEMON AND CAPER BUTTER

Obviously any chapter containing the story of the salmon of knowledge demands an accompanying salmon recipe. When eating fish I always feel vaguely virtuous and then invariably smother it in cream and white wine, but in a fit of restraint in this instance I opted for a shitload of butter, and it tastes delish. **Serves 2**

- 2 salmon fillets, skin on
- 2 tablespoons olive oil
- 2 tablespoons butter
- 1 garlic clove, finely chopped
- zest of ½ lemon
- 1 tablespoon lemon juice
- 1 tablespoon capers
- 1 tablespoon chopped parsley
- salt and freshly ground black pepper

Heat a non-stick frying pan over a high heat. Drizzle the salmon with the oil. Place the fillets in the pan, skin-side down, and cook for about 4 minutes until the skin is crispy and golden, then gently turn the fish and cook on the other side for 2–3 minutes.

Melt the butter in a separate small frying pan, then add the garlic and lemon zest and sauté to release the aromas. Stir in the lemon juice, capers and parsley. Serve with some sautéed leek or grilled asparagus and sweet potato mash (see page 58).

SWEET POTATO MASH

Mashed potato is about as comforting and as childhood evoking as food comes. It is the food that I always wish I had the wherewithal to make when I'm tired or hungover or just plain lazy. My ideal restaurant has mash listed among the sides. I am completely indiscriminatory when it comes to mash. I'll eat it smooth, lumpy, creamy, cheesy, buttery and even cold. This sweet and delicately spiced mash is the perfect foil for the sharp and deeply savoury fizz of capers and lemon. It's a foolproof method also, as boiling potatoes can often make them lose their shit and become sodden. **Serves 2**

- 4 tablespoons cream
- 4 tablespoons butter
- ½ teaspoon ground nutmeg
- 800g sweet potatoes, peeled and cubed
- salt and freshly ground black pepper

Combine the cream, butter and nutmeg in a saucepan over a medium heat. Add the chunks of sweet potato and cover with a lid. Cook for about 20 minutes until the potato is tender. Mash and stir in salt and pepper to taste.

ULTIMATE CHILLI

Like mash, chilli was another staple of childhood dinners and to this day one of my absolute faves. The chilli was a stalwart in my dad's repertoire. Like myself he had a talent for melting cheese, a once-a-generation cheese-melting talent – but beyond that he was a good cook, so it is going to sound like I am slightly overstating his talents as a cook when I say that the secret ingredient to his famous chilli was ketchup, which is perhaps not the most innovative secret ingredient of all time. This version of chilli pushes the boat out somewhat with ale, coffee and chocolate for a rich, deeply unctuous sauce. **Serves 4–6**

- 2 tablespoons rapeseed oil
- 2 onions, diced
- 3 garlic cloves, sliced
- 500g fresh beef mince
- 300g beef steak, cubed
- 2 tablespoons ground cumin
- 2 tablespoons ground coriander
- 2 teaspoons cayenne pepper
- 2 teaspoons dried oregano
- 400g tinned chopped tomatoes
- 400ml dark ale
- 50ml espresso coffee
- 2 tablespoons tomato purée
- 2 tablespoons tomato ketchup
- 2 squares plain chocolate
- 1 tablespoon dark brown sugar
- 400g tinned red kidney beans
- 1–2 teaspoons salt
- soured cream and guacamole, to serve

Heat the oil in a large saucepan over a medium heat. Add the onions and garlic and cook until softened. Increase the heat and add the mince and steak and cook until browned all over.

Add the cumin, coriander, cayenne pepper and oregano, stir together and cook for about 5 minutes.

Add the tomatoes, ale, coffee, tomato purée and ketchup. Bring to the boil, then simmer for 30–45 minutes until the sauce has thickened.

Drain the beans and stir into the chilli with the chocolate and sugar. Check the seasoning with 1–2 teaspoons of salt and serve with soured cream and guacamole.

Sassy Chilli

CHAPTER 4

Eating – a life's work

In which I attempt to eat

ALL the sweets and chocolates and biscuits

and butter and ice cream and Twixes, and

EXPLORE THE GREED that has fuelled

my every decision since the first time I

tasted a two-finger KitKat.

OBVIOUSLY I'VE BEEN EATING ALL MY LIFE, WE ALL HAVE. BUT I'M NOT SURE IF everybody else is quite so consumed with the task of feeding themselves as I am. A question I like to ask people when I'm interviewing them is 'What is that last thing you think about at night before going to sleep?' To this day, either nobody has ever answered this question honestly, or I am literally the only person in the world who drifts off to sleep musing on the following day's menu plan.

By the time I'm lying in bed and that gentle tug breaks the thread that moors us to wakefulness, there is a little smile playing on my lips. Not because, as some of my interviewees have answered, I am thinking about my loved ones or, indeed, some irksome task that was satisfactorily accomplished that day. It's because I am planning the butternut squash and poached eggs that I intend to make for breakfast.

Ah, breakfast. I am utterly obsessed by breakfast. If through some unforeseen series of calamities I happen to miss breakfast I always have to squeeze it in at some later point in the day. I don't see it as an event that passes and that is that. To me it is an essential stop on the day's journey, just as lunch is a pleasant pit stop on the way to dinner. If one or other of these culinary detours is encroached on by pesky obligations or external forces, I don't drop them from the itinerary – I just reschedule them.

Herself tells me that when I was a child I would keep a strict running tally of any meals that had fallen by the wayside and could never accept why, because I had missed breakfast the previous Tuesday, I couldn't cash it in now on Friday evening at 7.15. Even then, young as I was, I did realise that meal rescheduling couldn't go on indefinitely and I applied a sort of statute of limitations on revisiting missed meals. My policy (aged six) was that I had to consume the missed meal within the calendar week from which the meal was originally dropped.

My favourite breakfast as a child was a soft-boiled egg and soldiers with loads of butter. I liked (and to this day love) all kinds of eggs. I believe it was my love of eggs, coupled with my domineering and pedantic nature as a child, that set me on course eventually to become a cook. No one could cook my eggs the way I liked them. I tried in vain to correct my parents' abysmal efforts. My father erred on the side of undercooking, so that when presented with my egg I would have to conduct a detailed (and slightly passive aggressive) excavation of all filmy undercooked white that I considered to be disgusting and totally inedible. Meanwhile, Herself has that gift for overcooking everything that she applies heat to, from eggs to French beans – her French beans can be consumed through a straw.

I know that had I been born a couple of decades earlier I would been given a good educational slap and reminded of the starving children in Africa (which did on occasion happen when my Granny visited), but the notion that others exist apart from yourself when you are a cosseted and indulged and unbearably self-centred only child is just too abstract to take on. Never mind when the others in question are poor starving children in a far-flung place and, anyway, they shouldn't be subjected to undercooked egg white either, was my obnoxious reasoning.

Because my parents wouldn't take on board my constructive criticism I shouldered the burden of cooking my own breakfast and at that young age learned the valuable lesson (insert heavy, put-upon, six-year-old sigh), 'if you want something done right ...'

Herself noticed the burgeoning interest in cooking and bought me a Dorling Kindersley children's cookbook from which I subjected them to heinous concoctions like cheese, onion and potato pie (something that, of course, can be delicious, but not in the hands of this child – think undercooked onion with centimetre-thick slices of plastic early 1990s-style red Cheddar), tomato and orange soup (I did not possess the flair to pull this one off) and leaden, inedible loaves of bread (I love making bread and to this day lack any real talent for it – luckily Himself is a great bread maker).

My early explorations in food relied heavily on melted cheese in much the same way that my current food mantra could be summed up as 'cook it in chorizo oil'. I displayed a precocious talent for melting cheese and was inventive with my many and varied snacks imagined through the medium of cheese.

Unsurprisingly, in my teens I once had gout. Herself was mortified and told me to tell everyone it was cellulitis. In my teenage wisdom I thought that something containing the word cellulite was far more embarrassing and instead went with the gout story. People think that gout is some kind of historical 'joke' ailment, but it is still out there, punishing lovers of rich food the world over.

My mate Fat Tits puts my getting gout down to the fact that as teenagers foraging for food in my parents' house (a house always stocked with an exotic array of condiments), we were often short a vehicle to purvey their fabulous condiment varietals to our mouths. Necessity is the mother of invention and soon I pioneered the cheese cracker. This is where one uses a thick slice of cheese in place of a traditional cracker and leads to such atrocities as a slice of cheese being used to convey pâté and cream cheese to the mouth, and, of course, gout.

I've always been fascinated by people who seem wholly unconcerned with food. The kind of people who forget they've got a bar of chocolate in their bag, for example. Or the people who aren't sure what's for dinner. It baffles me. I often wonder how I would expend all the extra mental energy I would have if only I wasn't consumed with thoughts of food. As a child I was one of those kids who, upon arriving at someone's house, could detect an unopened packet of crisps in a drawer 20 feet away. And I wouldn't be at peace until I was eating them.

Recently I was reminiscing with a friend about going to her house to play when we were kids. I began to wax on about the incredible sweets that were always available there. Her mother would produce a large Tupperware box that was always generously stocked with two-finger Kit Kats and Wagon Wheels. Even at that young age I remember looking at my friend's family, who were all of average height and build, and thinking how? How were they not fat? How did they not have to replenish that Tupperware box every single day?

In my house there were no treats, no biscuit tin and no Tupperware of two-finger Kit Kats. This was most definitely a mistake on the part of Herself. She was obviously trying to be healthy and keep me (and my dad, most likely) away from sugar. What she didn't count on was the fact that by depriving me of 'nicies' (as we called them in our house), she was in fact fetishising them. That box would never have been allowed in our house and had it been I wouldn't have had a moment's rest until its contents were completely demolished.

Herself clearly recognised that she was living with two compulsive personalities. My dad was definitely a bit of a co-conspirator in the quest for nicies. Anytime Herself went away I could be sure that tasty treats would materialise throughout the house, and they would then have to be eaten rapidly and all evidence disposed of before her return.

I am particularly greedy when it comes to sweets. Societal pressure demands that I pretend I want to share confectionery with others, but in fact, from a young age, I deeply resented this. I soon devised a strategy that enabled me to 'share' my treats with the other children, but ensured that I didn't lose out too much in the process. I would exclusively choose sweets that came in individual, tiny portions, such as packets of Rolos or Munchies.

I found these much more conducive to sharing than, say, a Mars bar or a Snickers. This is because, when sharing a chocolate bar, you run the risk of breaking off far more than you initially intended in the sharing transaction. This is the worst, as any attempt to re-break the bar will result in looks of disgust from your contemporaries, and a bar that is now virtually inedible due to manhandling.

The other strategy I devised as a child to avoid the mandatory sharing was to purchase confectionery items that require full-on mouth-to-item contact – your Creme Eggs, your Walnut Whips – unsightly sucking is a great deterrent to the would-be grabbers. Sadly, one of my favourite indulgences is a Bounty, which is highly conducive to sharing with others, as it comes not as a single bar but as two mini bars. Just try and open a Bounty in a one-on-one scenario without capitulating to the pressure of social norms and offering your companion the other half – it cannot be done.

It is probably not that surprising, given my obsession with food, that one of the single most traumatic events during my childhood involved a Twix. Now, just a reminder that you didn't buy this book to read about my abusive childhood or how I escaped a war zone aged 10. This book isn't called *A Girl Called It*. So, you know, remember the trauma bar for me – the child of two loving parents raised in Dublin in the 1990s – is not that high. But even on the scale of personal trauma, really the Twixident shouldn't in all seriousness get top billing. Surely the time I saw a flasher at Booterstown DART station, or the time, aged 12, a passing stranger groped my barely-there breast at a concert, or at the very least the numerous times I inadvertently witnessed parental copulation, should all rank higher in my tally of early childhood trauma, but, no, it was the Twix.

It was a Friday when I was about seven and Herself and I were supposed to be going to Cork for the weekend. I was to be picked up in a taxi and brought to where my mother was working. This part of the plan failed completely. My uncle, who had put me in the taxi, had neglected to tell the taxi driver where to go. After a few minutes' driving the taxi driver turned and asked (quite reasonably), 'Where to?' This totally stumped me, I didn't know 'where to'. It didn't occur to my seven-year-old brain to go back to my house and ask my uncle to clarify. So, after a few minutes' thinking, I suggested we go to my mother's office.

When we reached her office, her colleague said that she was out on location filming. So we proceeded to the address given to us by the colleague. When we got there my mother was beside herself. She was at once reeling from terror at my failure to appear at the appointed time and furious because as a result of our detour we were now running late for the Cork train. She jumped in the taxi and we sped to the station.

It was one of those perplexing times when someone's fear neatly turns to fury as soon as the perceived danger is no longer a threat. All the intensity that she had been feeling when she thought that I was taken from her, gone for ever, was now redirected into blaming me for the train that we were about to miss.

As a mother now I totally understand this. Your children can elicit emotions so potent in you that you literally don't know where to put them. This invariably leads to this kind of irrational reaction and, later, an unproductive and illogical self-berating. As the proud owner of a child, I can also recognise how lucky I am to have actually survived what happened next.

As we were running to the train I dropped my penny jar. The jar that I would have to have tucked under my jacket for absolutely no reason whatsoever, because I was seven and that is exactly the kind of thing seven-year-olds prioritise when there's a train to catch and only minutes to spare. It was an old Nescafé jar filled with coppers that smashed spectacularly upon making contact with the ground. Money and glass went everywhere.

My mother came to a dead stop and wheeled around with an absolutely terrifying expression on her face. In my memory her eyes turned fully black. She summoned some inner reserves of restraint and managed to produce a sinister and most unnatural-looking smile for the benefit of the surrounding onlookers.

To those around us she was a harried mother taking a sudden child-caused setback with a wry smile and commendable patience. To me she was the woman gripping my wrist and presumably about to kill me. We missed the train.

With our train gone, the mess cleared up and a few hours to kill, Herself and I went to the train station coffee shop. Herself got a coffee and a Twix and proceeded to slowly and methodically consume the Twix in front of me without offering me a single bite. How could something so delicious be so malicious? How could something I love so much cause me so much pain?

It is a testament to my obsession with food that in a story where I found myself alone in a taxi with no idea where I was going it is the Twix consumption that really stayed with me. This 'trauma' is also further testament to the charmed childhood I had.

Herself will go absolutely spare when she finds out that the Twixident made it into these pages, especially as she spent my entire childhood pandering to my every whim, but what can I say? That early betrayal had a profound effect on me. It was the first time I realised that we humans are capable of inflicting pain for the sheer satisfaction of revenge. For Herself, exhausted from a long week's work, facing into a weekend with her own mother (with all the attendant aggression that brings) and thwarted by an infuriating seven-year-old, I still wonder how that Twix tasted. Was it ashes in her mouth or, as it seemed to me, delicious?

BOUNTY TRUFFLES

These bounty truffles neatly address that pesky issue of feeling pressured into sharing your Bounty bar. And they taste delicious. Side note: ANYTHING involving condensed milk is ace in my book. The day I discovered pouring condensed milk on porridge was a good day, and I'm convinced that the health properties of porridge cancel out the condensed milk. **Makes about 24**

200ml tinned condensed milk
- *240g white chocolate*
- *1 tablespoon butter*
- *120g desiccated coconut*
- *300g plain chocolate, for coating*

Line two baking trays with baking paper and set aside. Put the condensed milk, white chocolate and butter into a saucepan and heat over a low heat until the chocolate and butter are melted, stirring until smooth and creamy, then add the coconut and mix well.

Leave to cool in the pan for about 10 minutes at room temperature, then spoon about 12 generous tablespoons of the mixture onto each of the prepared trays, leaving plenty of space between each pile. Chill in the fridge for 30 minutes.

Meanwhile, put the plain chocolate into a heatproof bowl set over a saucepan of gently simmering water and heat, stirring frequently, until melted. Remove from the heat and leave to cool slightly. Take the coconut truffles out of the fridge. Roll each one in your hand to shape it into a small round ball, then replace it on the tray and press down lightly to give it a flat base.

Carefully spoon the plain chocolate over each truffle, ensuring that the sides are coated, then return them to the fridge for up to 1 hour, or until they are completely set.

KALE, TAHINI AND POACHED EGGS WITH ROAST SQUASH

This dish is one that I fall asleep fantasising about most nights. It's also a great incentive for me to get out of bed. Every week I roast a few squash on a Sunday or Monday night to see me through the week as a quick side for eggs or chilli or to bulk out a soup or curry. Butternut squash would definitely be on my desert island list of food. I reckon a lot of people avoid using squash because they think the chopping is a faff, but this method of roasting them is no effort at all and it gives the skin a nice caramelised finish. Tahini is also a storecupboard essential for me, and this simple dressing goes on about half the meals I eat – it's great with roast vegetables, halloumi, lamb, everything. **Serves 2**

- *1 butternut squash, halved lengthways and deseeded*
- *generous pinch of dried chilli flakes*
- *2 large handfuls of kale, stalks removed*
- *1 tablespoon olive oil*
- *juice of ½ lemon*
- *2 generous teaspoons tahini*
- *pinch of salt*
- *1 small garlic clove, crushed*
- *4–6 tablespoons water*
- *2 tablespoons white wine vinegar*
- *4 eggs*
- *sea salt and freshly ground black pepper*

Preheat the oven to 200°C/Gas 6. Pierce the thick necks of the squash halves with a knife a few times, then place both halves flesh-side down in a baking dish. Season with the chilli flakes, sea salt and pepper and bake in the preheated oven for 45 minutes or until tender. Remove from the oven and cut the squash flesh into chunks.

Place the kale, oil and lemon juice in a bowl and massage for about 5 minutes until the ingredients are well combined and the kale is bright green in colour.

Place the tahini, a pinch of salt and the garlic in a small bowl and gradually add the water, whisking until the mixture has the consistency of pouring cream. Add to the kale and toss to coat. Divide the kale mixture between two large bowls and add the squash.

Fill a medium-sized saucepan with boiling water, add the vinegar and bring to the boil. Reduce the heat slightly, swirl the water with a slotted spoon and then carefully drop in the eggs. Cook for 3–4 minutes, or to your liking. You can check them by lifting them out of the water with the slotted spoon after about 2 minutes and gently prodding the yolks. Place the eggs on top of the kale and squash and serve immediately.

HOME-MADE ROLOS

Home-made Rolos make a lovely gift ... to yourself. It's not until you make this caramel that you will realise that all the other synthetic, uninspiring caramels you've wasted your time eating over the course of a lifetime were terrible. Tasting this caramel for the first time is like when you fall in love with someone and realise that every other person you ever kissed was a hideous mistake. I can never get through making a batch of these without burning my tongue trying to eat the caramel while it's still hot. Every. Single. Time. But so so worth it. Note the condensed milk making a reappearance. If condensed milk were a person I would abandon my current family and elope with it.

Makes about 20 (depending on the size of your mould)

- 165ml tinned condensed milk
- ½ tablespoon golden syrup
- 30g butter
- 200g plain chocolate

You will also need:
- a chocolate mould in your preferred shape

Put the condensed milk, golden syrup and butter into a saucepan and heat over a medium heat, stirring constantly to prevent sticking. Cook the mixture – which will start out quite pale and liquid – until it is golden in colour and thick enough to draw a figure of eight on the surface several times without it disappearing. Remove the caramel from the heat and leave to cool.

Put the chocolate into a heatproof bowl set over a saucepan of very gently simmering water. Heat, stirring occasionally, until melted. Remove from the heat and leave to cool to room temperature, making sure that it doesn't begin to set.

Carefully spoon the melted chocolate into the chocolate moulds, then pour off the excess chocolate, ensuring that the sides of the moulds are well coated. Keep the leftover melted chocolate warm. Leave the moulds to set completely before gently spooning in the caramel filling, then spoon over a little of the remaining chocolate to cover the filling and seal the chocolates.

* I like to serve these guys straight from the fridge, mixed in a bowl of salty popcorn with a good movie – usually one starring Nicolas Cage. I have no taste!

CHAPTER 5

~~Denial~~

In which I recall my

VARIOUS NEUROTIC ATTEMPTS

to quell my compulsive eating tendencies

since I was a fat teenager (see Chapter 4).

ALL MY LIFE I HAVE ADORED EATING. FROM TIME TO TIME MY RELATIONSHIP WITH food has veered into dysfunctional territory. I think this is because I come from a long line of food neurotics. Growing up in my house we sat down to family dinner every night, but rarely did we all eat the same dishes. Everyone was on his or her own personal diet. My mother would be on the salmon and salad, keeping a running tally of her 'points' as she went. My aunts and cousins were always on the Hay or the South Beach, while my father was a devotee of a niche French doctor's rather prescriptive eating plan that called for a lot of red meat, red wine and dark chocolate. The only nod to health discernible from his diet was a fatwa on carrots due to their high sugar content.

The doctor in question was Michel Montignac, and he changed my father's whole approach to eating. I'm pretty sure Montignac didn't actually recommend the vast quantities of dark chocolate that my father consumed, but it has to be said, chocolate aside, under the good doctor's tutelage my dad lost an enormous amount of weight. By today's health-conscious fundamentalism I'm sure that BM (before Montignac) my dad would've been diagnosed as clinically obese. Back then, however, I think he was regarded more as having a healthy amount of 'joie de vivre', as evidenced by the wine and food that he consumed with abandon.

When he decided to shed the weight he approached it with the same zeal and commitment that he had once applied to consuming roast potatoes. Every man is Clint Eastwood in the film of his own life and I think it came as a bit of a shock to him when he hit his 40s and the reflection in the mirror bore absolutely no resemblance whatsoever to his celluloid hero. At some point he had begun to resemble more closely one of the bumbling, hopelessly uncool, unnamed small-time crooks that Dirty Harry neatly dispatches in the first few minutes of the film. The guys who, if they even made it into the credits, were probably referred to by unflattering monikers like 'Fat Guy 2' and 'Clumsy Con 4'. This did not marry up with my dad's Clint aspirations.

It was a particularly hard reality for him to grasp as he was a very good-looking man. I don't rely on memory with its subjective and unreliable nature to know this about him. On an almost weekly basis people who knew my father tell me this about him, as if this fact makes his current predicament all the sadder (see Chapter 18), which in a way it does. For example, Kevin was the proud and supremely vain owner of an exceptional tan, and in light of the relatively low percentage of naturally occurring tans in the Irish population it does seem terribly unfair that one of our best tanners should have been taken from us while still in his tanning prime.

Photographic evidence from the early 1970s suggests that not only did he possess an incredible 'colour', but also naturally blond hair and a rakish personal style somewhat out of sync with his native Cork. A souvenir from his first trip to Paris was a pair of flamboyant pink flares, which, if his account was to be believed, caused near riots on Saturday nights 'doing Pana', which translates from the Corkese as 'walking up and down St Patrick's Street'. Kev possessed the unshakeable self-assurance to carry off just such a divisive sartorial statement. Further testament to this: The man could rock a hat.

So you can understand the shock he must have felt when in his 40s his body was subsumed by the body of a man who could never wear a linen shirt unbuttoned to the waist while lounging in a polaroid from 1978 (this one's on my fridge). With a determination previously reserved for extracting every last scrap of meat from an animal carcass, Kev ditched carbs, embraced Montignac and hit the gym.

When working out he cultivated a sullen, prickly Clint-esque veneer of unapproachability to avoid having to chat to others while working out. He was not there to make friends, he was a lone wolf on a mission. Also, in an ambitious and impressive move, he'd elected to give up the secret smoking at the same time, so the no chatting could also have been a precautionary measure in case he should feel the urge to lash out at anyone trying to be chummy with him on the treadmills.

Watching a person make such a dramatic change to their lifestyle and appearance should have taught me a great lesson in the untold benefits of making healthy choices and having a balanced diet. But no, I remained resolutely fat from 1996 to 2009, even in the face of such concrete evidence telling me that taking a secret sandwich to bed every night was probably not the behaviour of a rational, healthy person.

In my early teens, with every passing year my dress size increased with my age. When I was 12, I was a size 12, when I was 14, a size 14, and so on. I never hit a dramatic size where I needed intervention beyond my mother endlessly trying to encourage me to eat more healthily and boys calling me fat, but in my head I was enormous. A lumbering, quivering, ugly mass. In other words, a pretty average teenage girl. I once read an incredibly relatable quote: 'I wish I was as fat as I was the first time I thought I was fat.'

We all care about diet these days. Nearly everyone I know has a pretty dysfunctional relationship with food. I'm not talking about people with actual mental illnesses, but the middle ground people who resolve week after week to do better and fail repeatedly, more often than not consoling themselves with a bottle of Châteauneuf-du-Pape and a slab of Délice de Bourgogne (I'm very specific in my consolatory treats, as you can see). Regarding my own dysfunctional relationship with food, I'm an all or nothing type. I can be found either bingeing on deep-fried Mars bars or weighing pieces of ham before consuming them with a few dry Ryvitas and a cherry tomato.

I always thought that I really envied people who could eat whatever they like without gaining an ounce, but I actually think if I were to suddenly develop a high-speed metabolism I would probably lose the will to do anything in life aside from eating. It's really only the fact that I can't eat 24 hours a day that means I get anything else done. Pursuing personal goals, maintaining inter-personal relationships and creating meaningful memories would all fall by the wayside if I could just lie around eating lime-flavoured Doritos and tzatziki all day and still get into my jeans. I'm just one of those people who is never too full for dessert, can finish a large popcorn in the cinema and still go for a meal afterwards and is genuinely baffled when someone describes a meal as 'too rich'. How could it be too rich? Surely that's like saying it was 'too delicious'.

When it comes to diets I was always a bit of a traditionalist. Diets that involve prehistoric lifestyle choices, large quantities of one particular ingredient, like apples or maple syrup, or bizarre and restrictive food pairings, such as only consuming carrots, raw, when the moon is waning, all baffle me.

But these days everyone has got their diet mantra. Mine was pretty retrograde. It's what I liked to think of as the 1990s approach, basically no carbs and lots of Diet Coke. I'd also go in for lots of fruit but now I find I am being lectured at parties by people who are sucking down e-cigarettes about how fruit is full of sugar. No comment.

However, as much as I like to think of myself as kind of immune to the diet trends, recently I got sucked in to the propaganda. I was sitting next to a girl who I'd noticed was in possession of an enviable physique. When canapés and drinks were offered round she declined and instead began sipping on a green drink she produced from her handbag.

'I'm on a juice cleanse,' she explained with a distinctly self-satisfied smile. She looked on disdainfully at the 'eaters' and serenely sipped. As much as I hate the thought of not eating I couldn't help but be intrigued. I got the run down. No solid food or caffeine for three days. As she expounded on the benefits with evangelical fervour, I began to picture myself feather-light, my skin clearer, the whites of my eyes whiter, and decided that the juice detox would invigorate me and offer untold health benefits.

I embarked on the detox on a Monday morning, kick-starting the day with a hot water and lemon followed by a green juice of unknown origin – I could've read the accompanying leaflet but by that stage my eyesight was already beginning to blur and an intense headache had set in. Not to mention a strange kind of low-grade yet all-pervading rage, which spiked occasionally at the most minor incidents.

Eight hours and two more juices later I was observing Himself cooking dinner while holding, just holding, I maintain, a morsel of chicken in my mouth. This proved too much for me and I proceeded to fall off the wagon in spectacular style, starting with the morsel of chicken, then falling upon the Kerrygold like a long-lost friend I had been mourning.

I now know that to undertake a juice detox one must have perfect conditions. Absolutely everything in your life must be running smoothly, because when the hunger kicks in so, too, does the rage. A juice detox on no sleep while caring for a nine-month-old baby and temporarily living in your mother's house are not the optimum conditions for fasting.

The juice cleanse taught me that I'm not really cut out for not eating. It also taught me that, in general, drinking my meals is deeply depressing. I need the chewing experience in order to feel satisfied, which is, of course, reasonable enough. One exception to this is my new penchant for drinking my breakfast in the form of a smoothie, which, on paper, is healthy, though I suspect that I'm doing it for all the wrong reasons. Also I think I'm taking the whole 'healthy fats' thing a tad too far, as about 30 per cent of my morning smoothie is almond butter, to mask the presence of kale and spinach. My suspect motivations are that I can now drink my breakfast while working in the morning. This kind of goes against the whole mindful eating movement, but for a perpetually late person like me, dispensing with chewing for at least one meal a day marginally improves my chaotic morning ritual.

As I said, I didn't really get the hang of the whole too-much-bad-food-equals-back-fat thing until relatively late in life. I continued on through my 20s eating like one of those people who have a really fast metabolism and can eat whatever they want, only I don't have a really fast metabolism and canNOT eat whatever I want. If all this obsessing about food and weight is a bit tiresome and predictable, I apologise. I hate this aspect of my personality. I hate conforming to a stereotype, especially such an uninspiring one as the 'woman obsessing over her weight' thing, but I think for me a far greater issue than how I actually look is the endless yo-yoing back and forth between 'being good' and 'being bad'. I can't seem to just 'be normal'. I am always either eating a fried cheese sandwich or sprinkling nutritional yeast all over everything and pretending it's cheese.

The lead-up to my wedding was probably the first time that I experienced at first hand what diet and exercise can do for a person. Conforming to another wearying stereotype I had, of course, embarked on the apparently mandatory pre-nuptial regime of manic weight loss. A friend of mine told me that a girl she knew kept saying in the lead-up to her wedding, 'I just want everyone to say, "My God, that bride is *too* thin".' I shuddered. 'Ugh, how awful,' I told my friend. But carried on obsessively cataloguing every scrap of calorie that I allowed past my lips none the less.

On the day of my wedding the same friend came rushing over to me and said (joking), 'Oh my God, that bride is too thin!' It was the first time in my life that I felt not fat. Not slim, just not fat. It is a true testament to the power of denial that even on the day of my wedding I still felt like my 14-year-old self poured into the body of a slim person. I once told a friend of mine that I am a fat person in a slim person's body. I think she called me a dickhead and laughed, but honestly it's how I feel. For the amount of purging, bingeing and obsessing over food that I do, you'd think I was enormous, and I don't even have a clinically diagnosed obsession. I'm just doing the same thing that millions of women of my generation are doing, eating salads all week, milling into a tub of ice cream at weekends and berating ourselves afterwards.

I look at my husband and marvel, actually marvel, at his lack of concern about what he eats. I observe him going about his day. Say it's a Saturday and there's no office to go to. He'll pop to the shop to get the paper and a pecan plait, which he will absentmindedly consume while reading the headlines, then I can almost hear the thoughts going through his head in the special caveman voice I always do for him. 'Still. Hungry. Need. More. Nom. Nom,' as he veers into the kitchen and prepares one of his patented heart-attack breakfasts, while I'm agonising over the nutritional information on a packet of rice cakes.

If we were to continue on the guided tour of Himself's culinary journey through the day there would be several more biscuit pit stops between breakfast and lunch, then a sandwich roughly the size of my head containing multiple meat products and vaguely clashing condiment combinations. The afternoon slump would be assuaged by tea and more biscuits. Then, as we are preparing dinner, he might be peckish. This is immediately remedied with a large bag of crisps, followed by the evening meal. It's quite a sight to behold.

Himself is obviously a big person. I don't know if he needs quite this quantity of food but he does manage to put it away and still retain a reasonably good shape. One thing I notice is that as much as he eats, he is still capable at times of declining the offer of food, and this may be where we differ. For all my neurotic cataloguing and compiling of calorie information, I am incapable of listening to my body and deciding when I'm full. It might be a mild form of Prader-Willi syndrome, if such a thing exists. Himself, on the other hand, for all his apparent gorging, has been known to utter the phrase, 'No thanks, I'm full.' Not something I'm ever likely to say.

After the settling down and the getting married bit I thought I might slack off on the whole neurotic food obsession. I was kind of banking on just letting myself go, now that I had somebody who was contractually obliged to fancy me regardless of weight gain or hair loss or disfigurement. But one marriage does not cure a lifetime of negative thinking. Perhaps my second marriage will, but in the meantime I began to consider some holistic intervention. Hypnosis always struck me as the ideal way to achieve any difficult task I've ever had to accomplish – the lazy person's remedy. However, my chronic laziness continues to prevent me tracking down a hypnotist and making an appointment.

Now that I am a bit older and my body has grown a person and all that, I feel that I am perhaps a little closer to getting a grip and accepting that I'm grand. My latest scheme is going to a mindfulness coach who specialises in breaking bad habits because, let's face it, I am boring myself to death thinking about eating all the time.

SWEET-AND-SOUR CHICKEN

A chapter that details my obsession with being 'good' wouldn't be complete without my favourite healthy(ish) dinners. I find once I get into the mindset of eating well I find it no hardship whatsoever. I think the most important part is making sure you're not punishing yourself with awful 'diet' food. Cottage cheese and the like (unless you actually like cottage cheese, in which case I fear that we have nothing in common and cannot be friends any more, because cottage cheese is disgusting). Being an enthusiastic and inventive eater has led me to masterminding healthier versions of my favourite foods (yes, they are all takeaways). After a satisfying yet healthy meal of turkey tacos I then feel free to drink all the wine and eat all the chocolate. It's a two steps forward, three steps backwards approach that keeps me always striving to lose those pesky three pounds ... which I can totally live with!

Sweet-and-sour chicken is such a guilty pleasure for me, I almost can't bring myself to order it – I feel like it's an affront to the lads in the local Chinese. Everyone else goes in there and orders the 'MegaBox' or sweet-and-sour chicken balls, and obviously I want to as well, but some part of me feels I've got something to prove to them: That I'm better than the average Chinese takeaway frequenter (which I'm not, clearly). I want to show them I have discerning tastes and a desire to sample more authentic Chinese takeaway offerings. Usually the deep-fryer gets the better of me and I get a three in one and go home to weep-eat while filled with self-loathing. This home-made sweet-and-sour chicken actually does manage to capture some of the takeaway version's down-and-dirty delicious baaaadness while not inspiring any self-loathing.

Serves 3 (or 2 really greedy people)

- 1 whole pineapple, peeled and centre discarded (blend half the pineapple with 200ml water and chop the other half into chunks.)
- juice of 1 grapefruit
- 1 red pepper, deseeded and thinly sliced
- 1 red chilli, deseeded and finely sliced
- 2 teaspoons Chinese five-spice powder
- 50g tamarind paste
- 40g caster sugar
- 100ml rice wine vinegar
- vegetable oil, for frying
- 2 large skinless chicken breasts, cut into bite-sized pieces
- pinch of salt
- 1 small onion, peeled and sliced into chunks
- 70g baby corn, roughly chopped
- 70g mangetout, roughly chopped
- cooked rice, to serve

Pour the blended pineapple through a sieve into a medium-sized saucepan (you should have about 300ml juice). Add the grapefruit juice, red pepper and sliced chilli to the pineapple juice, bring to the boil, then reduce the heat and simmer for 10 minutes. Blend in a food processor or with a hand-held blender.

Return the red pepper purée to the pan and add the pineapple chunks, five-spice powder, tamarind paste, sugar and vinegar. Simmer for 30 minutes, or until reduced and thick.

Heat a little oil in a wide non-stick saucepan over a medium heat. Add the chicken to the pan with the salt and stir-fry until the chicken is just cooked through. Add the onion and cook until the onion is slightly softened but still has a bit of bite. Add the baby corn and mangetout and cook until tender.

Pour in the sweet-and-sour sauce and stir together until well combined. Serve with cooked rice.

TURKEY TACOS
Serves 4

- 1 small onion
- 2 garlic cloves, peeled
- large handful of fresh coriander, stalks included
- juice of 2 limes
- ½ green chilli
- 2 tablespoons rapeseed oil
- 500g fresh turkey mince
- ½ teaspoon chilli powder
- ½ teaspoon ground cumin
- 1 teaspoon dried oregano
- 400g tinned whole peeled tomatoes
- 2 small heads of cos lettuce, leaves separated
- salt

Optional toppings:
- chunks of avocado
- jalapeños
- grated cheese
- soured cream

Blitz the onion, garlic, coriander, lime juice and green chilli in a food processor. Heat the oil in a non-stick frying pan over a medium heat. Add the turkey and fry for about 5 minutes until browned all over. Add the chilli powder, cumin, oregano and ½ teaspoon of salt and stir together.

Pour in the blitzed mixture and stir to combine. Cook for about 5 minutes until the turkey is cooked through. Add the tomatoes and roughly break up with a spatula. Increase the heat to medium–high and simmer for about 10 minutes until thickened.

Check the seasoning, adding a little more salt if needed. Arrange the lettuce leaves on plates and top with the turkey mixture and any additional toppings. Serve immediately.

PAD THAI WITH COURGETTI

Pad Thai is a great gateway dish for cooking Thai. It's quick to prepare and tastes way too nice to be as healthy as it actually is. I originally worked out this alternative to the usual takeaway when I realised that my local Thai place was becoming way, way too familiar with particulars of my life. When the girl who takes the orders notices a new haircut, it's time to cut back. Or at the very least start alternating between the regular place and the place 10 minutes further away to throw them off your scent. This home-made version is a good approximation of the takeaway with some pretty virtuous updates. **Serves 2**

- *30ml Thai fish sauce*
- *1 teaspoon tamarind paste*
- *30ml water*
- *1 teaspoon brown sugar*
- *1 tablespoon groundnut oil*
- *2 chicken breasts, sliced*
- *pinch of dried chilli flakes*
- *juice of ½ lime*
- *2 garlic cloves, thinly sliced*
- *2 eggs*
- *100g broccoli, chopped quite small*
- *100g mangetout, roughly sliced*
- *1 carrot, peeled and julienned*
- *3 spring onions, sliced*
- *1 courgette, very finely sliced lengthways*
- *sea salt and freshly ground black pepper*
- *lime wedges and a handful of chopped roasted peanuts, to garnish*

Put the fish sauce, tamarind paste, water and sugar into a saucepan and bring to the boil to dissolve the sugar. Pour into a small cup and set aside.

Heat the oil in a frying pan over a high heat. Add the chicken to the pan with salt and pepper to taste, the chilli flakes and lime juice and cook, stirring, until the chicken is cooked through. Add the garlic and stir-fry for a couple of minutes.

Lightly beat the eggs with a fork in a bowl, then push all the chicken to the side of the pan, pour in the eggs and quickly scramble them with a spatula.

Mix the chicken into the scrambled egg, add the tamarind sauce and toss in the broccoli, mangetout, carrot and spring onions. Stir-fry for a few minutes until the broccoli is cooked to your liking.

Add the courgetti and toss everything together until the courgetti have softened. Transfer to warmed bowls, garnish with lime wedges and chopped peanuts and serve immediately.

FRIED CHICKEN

I was pretty sceptical of trying to healthify fried chicken. It's got 'fried' in the title, for God's sake, but this recipe really does capture the flavour and crunch pretty well. This is served with carrot chips as a kind of 'home fries' alternative. Add some slaw to save the plate from looking too much like a deep-fried platter. As a compromise I bake the whole lot, which is considerably better than frying and, happily, is also less of a palaver. As for the barbecue sauce, if I had to pick just one condiment for the rest of my life (I have something of a condiment fixation), it would have to be this sauce. Or Dijon mustard. Or mayonnaise. Or tartare. Or curried mayo. No, I take it back – I can't pick just one, it's like choosing to save just one pair of shoes from a fire – please just don't put me in that position. **Serves 2**

- 6–8 large carrots, cut into thin sticks
- ½ teaspoon dried chilli flakes (optional)
- 1 tablespoon clear honey
- olive oil, for coating
- 100ml milk
- 1 tablespoon lemon juice
- 1 egg white
- 2 skinless chicken breasts, each cut into 3 pieces lengthways
- 60g self-raising flour

- 2 teaspoons salt
- 2 teaspoons dried oregano
- 2 teaspoons chilli powder
- 1 garlic clove, crushed
- cooking spray
- sea salt flakes and freshly ground black pepper

Preheat the oven to 200°C/Gas 6. Toss the carrots with the chilli flakes, honey and just enough olive oil to coat.

Spread the sticks on a baking sheet in a single layer and sprinkle with sea salt and pepper. Bake on the upper rack of the preheated oven for 45 minutes, tossing halfway through cooking, until slightly charred and crisp.

Meanwhile, combine the milk and lemon juice in a bowl and leave to stand for a couple of minutes, then whisk in the egg white and add the chicken pieces. In a separate bowl mix together the flour, salt, oregano, chilli powder and garlic.

Line a grill tray with foil, then spray the grill rack with cooking spray to minimise sticking during cooking. Turn the chicken in the milk mixture to coat fully, then transfer the pieces one at a time to the flour mixture and turn to coat evenly. Arrange the chicken pieces on the grill rack and mist with a little cooking spray. Bake in the oven for 30 minutes until golden and crispy.

* You can make the carrot chips in advance and then crisp them in a hot oven for about 10 minutes just before serving.

LAZY NO-COOK BBQ SAUCE

When Himself and I met, I saw in him a kindred condiment spirit.

Our mutual obsession was even commemorated in a touching speech at our wedding given by a close friend of ours, who likened me to mayonnaise, Himself to ketchup and our union to Marie Rose sauce. Himself was dying to dub this tangy home-made condiment Himself's Special Sausage Jam (sorry for the mental image).

Luckily, I prevailed, and it was known henceforth by this more modest moniker.

Makes about 4 cups

- *300g dark brown sugar*
- *300g tomato ketchup*
- *4 tablespoons balsamic vinegar*
- *1 tablespoon Worcestershire sauce*
- *2 ½ teaspoons American mustard*
- *2 teaspoons smoked paprika*
- *salt and freshly ground black pepper, to taste*

Whisk all the ingredients together. BAM. DONE.

CHAPTER 6

Food to eat when you're **fat**

In which I celebrate the pure, unadulterated joy of EATING BISCUITS IN BED, and reconcile myself to the fact that I may never be capable of restraint in the face of deliciousness.

AS I MENTIONED PREVIOUSLY IN THESE PAGES, I'VE BEEN PRETTY FAT AT TIMES IN my life. If I'm honest, I think my natural state is a state of chunkiness. Every now and then I manage to whittle myself down to about a size 10, but the effort this requires is too great and invariably I throw myself into eating again until I'm back where I started. I liken this sensation to that of diving under water, kicking and flailing in a bid to stay submerged. Though in my imagination this scenario takes place in a vat of melted butter. You know you can touch the bottom, but giving up and resurfacing is kind of inevitable, at which point, defeated, I proceed to drink the butter. God, I love butter.

Being a fat teenager is a fairly crap position to be in. At no other time in life do we find ourselves surrounded by such a concentration of assholes than when we are in secondary school. It really is most unfortunate that we have to attend school with our peers, especially when our peers are in the throes of hormonal rages and liable to lash out at whomsoever appears the weakest (or chubbiest).

Of course I do feel huge relief that I was in secondary school 15 years ago, before social media, high-def make-up, selfies and 'thinspiration'. At least back then everyone, even the 'hot' girls, looked kind of shit. Mercifully, cut-off shorts and stripper heels and bandage dresses were not yet a part of our lexicon. Generally, the Bitch Herd were swathed in fleece, with baggy sweat pants providing coverage for our pasty, chunky legs. To the opposite sex our gender was barely discernible, never mind any level of hotness, and this protected our delicate teenage egos to a certain extent.

For me, being fat was just an immutable fact of life. I don't know whether it was just the kind of girl I was, or whether the Bitch Herd or our generation was perhaps just a shade less obsessed with dieting and fitness than these days. I didn't read *Seventeen* or *More* magazine. I didn't think that using *slices* of butter on toast had any correlation to having trouble finding a pair of parachute pants that fit. All I know is that I moaned sporadically about being fat but would also, virtually in the same breath, panic because I thought I'd dropped my king-sized Mars bar somewhere.

Being a fat teenager did do me a few favours. For example I didn't have sex until I was at least 18. Phew. Kept that vagina under wraps (or flesh folds more like) for years. It saved me from having any expectations of boys and therefore from being disappointed by them. It also means that, mercifully, there is little to no photographic evidence of me in swimming togs prior to 2009. My friend Jenga and I once went to France when we were 16 and, to the bemusement of our host family, we went swimming at the beach in leggings and oversized T-shirts, such was our commitment to keeping our grotesque bodies out of sight. If only I could have the body of my 16-year-old self back now, dammit.

Of course a big part of the problem was that I viewed eating as a kind of sport and, in addition to this, I didn't play any actual sport, which might have counter-balanced things somewhat. My all-time favourite pastime then, and to this day, is eating in bed while reading a book. Unfortunately, salads do not lend themselves to being consumed one-handed while lying in bed reading *Harry Potter*. Do you know what does lend itself to this activity? Sandwiches. And popcorn. And crisps. And anything from the biscuit family, really.

There's really no greater luxury than lying in bed when you are perfectly well. If I could travel back in time I would revisit one of those afternoons of heavy gestating. I would spend the day in bed eating and reading and moaning (pleasure whingeing, really) and delighting in my sheer volume. Kind people told me that I was very 'neat', and other weird comments that, for some reason, we as a society have deemed complimentary to the heifer-like incubators that lumber among us heroically expanding the species.

I had one friend who, every time she saw me pregnant, would shout, 'My God, you're huge!' I quickly came to hate her, but now I get what she was trying to do. She was taking back all the 'glowing' and 'neatness' and bullshit that we put on pregnant women about 'styling their bumps', and 'bouncing back' and 'milfing about in lululemon'. She was saying, 'You're huge, you're massive', in the grandest, most goddamn impressive sense of the thing; you're only massive. That's the mad thing about pregnancy fat, it's the female body pretty much fulfilling its biological destiny, getting to its physiological conclusion. This is my theory on why so many women look almost celestially divine in their big, sweaty, gloriously fat fullness of pregnancy. Of course I'm speaking in generalisations here, and some pregnancies are hellish. And also I'm pretty sure I didn't look remotely divine. I looked more like Philip Seymour Hoffman crossed with a sweaty gammon ham.

These days being fat or thin or just a woman of any kind, really, can be turned into a bit of a political battleground. At first, when writing 'The Domestic', I tried to mask my rabid obsession with bingeing, purging and dieting, as nothing ruins food and cooking quite like guilt. And I was also hating the fact that I'm such a goddamn stereotype. But then I became irritated with myself for being in denial, and about my preoccupation with denial.

It didn't seem particularly honest to pretend that I eat fried sandwiches all the time with absolutely no hang-ups. I have at least given

up loathing my body with the vehemence I possessed as a teenager. Now I just get on with things. I lug it around with me, occasionally irritated at how cumbersome it is, but recognising that I can hardly ply it with cheese and then expect it to be streamlined and firm. Now I am more accepting of my pattern, I accept that 'being good' and 'being bad' might just be too ingrained a part of my personality to change at this stage. And I'm a reasonably sized individual. Himself isn't searching through rolls of flab trying to find my vagina, nor does he ever mistake a particularly high up tummy roll for a boob, so I have to believe that I'm doing reasonably okay.

Unfortunately, not wanting to be fat can easily be construed as fat-shaming in this easily outraged society of ours. So, let me be clear, I don't care if you are fat. I just care if I am fat. Because for me being fat isn't a nice feeling – I know because I've been pretty fat. And being fat is not very healthy.

Having said that, as part of a 'balanced', 'healthy' lifestyle, I occasionally throw myself with total abandon into eating. It's a pleasure. I have at least ceased to see it as a sport (though I reckon I could eat anyone under the table) or pastime, but as more of a joy. When I'm in the right mood I'll just take the pants off and go for it. My motto now, though, is, if I'm going to eat the shit out of something then it'd better be worth it. It'd better be outrageously delicious.

Before reaching this state of (admittedly dubious) enlightenment I coined a phrase: rage-eating. Rage-eating is a bit like hate-watching. It's indulging in something that is not bettering you remotely but is still oddly satisfying and definitely compulsive. For example, I love hate-watching the *Twilight* movies or hate-reading trashy celebrity magazines. Both activities are irritating but pleasurable, driven by some irresistible inner force. Hate-watching usually occurs with lowbrow entertainment.

Likewise, rage-eating usually strikes with food that invariably contains little to no nutritional value or requires no special effort of preparation in order to consume vast quantities in a short space of time. The family-sized bag of chocolates or the jumbo bag of crisps, for example. You know this one, right? You buy the bag to last the week. You open it for a taster before popping it back in the press. You go and have a sit and try not to think about it. Then dissatisfaction sets in. You go back for a few more bites. Then you ignore the bag for a while, pretend to be doing a few jobs, call a friend, try to live a normal life. All in vain. With each pointless task you set yourself in the kitchen, you delve in for another little morsel.

Then the rage sets in. 'Damn it,' you think, 'I've gone this far.' And, inevitably, you snatch up the bag, assume some grotesque animalistic position and systematically devour every last morsel. Only when the item has been consumed can you relax, but the rest period is brief, as what quickly follows is a skewed kind of eater's remorse. This remorse is not really about greed or lack of self-control but about wasting a good bout of rage-eating on shitty old own-brand sweets or MSG-laden snacks. My attitude is that I should have committed myself to greed earlier and stocked up on better food. Each time I vow that in future I will not be squandering an opportunity for rage-eating on any old crap, instead I'll be reserving my glorious gorging for seriously decadent eats.

FRENCH TOAST WITH BACON
AND MAPLE SYRUP ICE CREAM

Very, very occasionally Himself gets on a healthy eating jag. Allow me to set the scene. It is 3.30 in the morning. The floor is littered with the detritus of a drunkenly conceived takeaway. Himself is on the couch and has assumed a position that in our house we call Level 10.

Don't be getting excited now, there is nothing remotely amorous about Level 10. It is the final stage of sitting before you could be considered supine. The chin is resting on the chest, limp arms lie beside the torso – which is occupying the seat portion of the couch as opposed to the usual back section – and the legs trail lifelessly to the floor.

'I'm starting boot camp,' he announces.

I respond incredulously: 'You just complimented the girl in Luigi's on her new haircut, meaning you know the staff of our local takeaway well enough to keep track of their hairstyles.'

'Shmalls the moor paison,' he says, which I interpret as 'all the more reason'. Immediately, I know that he must be stopped. Improved diet and exercise leads to more energy, and for the sake of our marriage I need to keep him doughy and lethargic – and probably not use these adjectives to describe him. No one can resist this frankly outrageous breakfast of ice cream and bacon. **Serves 2**

Ice cream

- *500ml cream*
- *200ml milk*
- *200ml tinned condensed milk*
- *5 cloves*
- *100ml maple syrup*
- *1 bay leaf*
- *1 teaspoon grated nutmeg*
- *5 egg yolks*
- *30g caster sugar*

French toast

- *3 eggs*
- *125ml milk*
- *lots of butter, for cooking (no point in holding back on this one, you're already eating ice cream for breakfast)*
- *4 thick slices of good white bread*
- *lots of crispy bacon, to serve*

To make the ice cream, put the cream, milk, condensed milk, cloves, maple syrup, bay leaf and nutmeg into a saucepan and bring to the boil, then remove from the heat and leave to infuse for 15 minutes.

Meanwhile, whisk the egg yolks with the sugar for 4 minutes until the mixture is very pale and has the consistency of whipped cream. Pour the cream-and-milk mixture into the egg mixture through a sieve, then stir to combine. Pour this custard-like mixture into a clean saucepan and heat over a medium heat, stirring constantly, until it is thick enough to coat the back of a spoon. Leave to cool, pour it into a container and place it in the freezer.

Over the next 2–3 hours take the ice cream out of the freezer every 30 minutes or so and stir well to break up the ice crystals. A hand-held blender is good for this, and an ice-cream maker is even better, if you have one.

When your ice cream is ready it is time for 'Operation Plumpington' (making the French toast) to commence. Whisk the eggs and milk together until combined. Melt about a tablespoon of butter in a non-stick frying pan over a medium–high heat. Dip the slices of bread in the egg mixture and then fry until golden and crispy on both sides. Serve the French toast with the bacon and ice cream.

CHOCOLATE CHIP COOKIES

I love whipping up a batch of these delicious shortbread chocolate-chip cookies. They are worth the tiny bit of effort that goes into making them – a bit of effort that may actually curb my compulsion to devour them all in one sitting and enjoy them instead. **Makes 15**

- 250g butter
- 115g icing sugar
- 400g plain flour
- 250g plain chocolate chips

Preheat the oven to 160°C/Gas 3. Line two baking sheets with greaseproof paper.

Put the butter and sugar into a bowl and beat together until pale and fluffy, then add the flour and beat to a soft dough. Add the chocolate chips and mix through.

Divide the dough into 15 pieces and shape each piece into a ball, place on the lined baking sheets and, using the palm of your hand, flatten each one slightly. Bake in the preheated oven for 15 minutes until lightly browned.

Leave to cool and dry out on the baking sheet.

PEANUT BUTTER AND WHITE CHOCOLATE COOKIES

Makes about 30–40 large cookies – or biscuits, as Himself insists on calling them.

- *200g crunchy peanut butter*
- *125g butter, softened*
- *150g caster sugar*
- *175g soft brown sugar*
- *2 teaspoons vanilla extract*
- *1 egg*
- *100g oats, blended into a fine 'flour'*
- *1 teaspoon bicarbonate of soda*
- *125g rolled oats*
- *100g white chocolate drops*

Preheat the oven to 160°C/Gas 3. Line four baking trays with baking paper. Put the peanut butter, butter, caster sugar, brown sugar, vanilla extract and egg into a bowl and beat until the mixture is creamy and well combined. Add the oat 'flour', bicarbonate of soda, rolled oats and chocolate drops and beat until a dough forms.

For each cookie, spoon out about a 30-g piece of dough. Place 9 pieces of dough on each baking tray, spaced well apart to allow for spreading during baking.

Bake the cookies in batches in the middle of the preheated oven for about 10–15 minutes, or until golden around the edges and lightly coloured on top. Leave to cool in the trays for at least 20 minutes, then transfer to a wire rack to cool completely. The cookies should be crunchy on the outside and nice and chewy in the centre.

You can cook half the dough and roll the remainder into a sausage shape, wrap it in baking paper and clingfilm, then store it in the fridge or freezer for future use.

DEEP-FRIED MARS BARS

This is a nod to my adolescent self. The Bitch Herd was never tempted by a deep-fried Mars bar, but we were always threatening to give them a go until finally my curiosity got the better of me. The result? Not as sickening as you'd expect … in fact, dangerously nice. **Makes 10–12**

- *125g self-raising flour*
- *130ml milk*
- *1 egg*
- *¼ teaspoon salt*
- *sunflower oil, for frying*
- *10–12 fun-sized Mars bars*
- *vanilla ice cream, to serve*

Place the flour, milk, egg and salt in a bowl and whisk thoroughly to make a smooth, fairly thick batter.

Pour oil to a depth of 5cm into a small saucepan and heat over a medium heat for about 5 minutes, or until a drop of the batter sizzles and immediately pops back to the surface when dropped into the pan.

Dip each Mars bar into the batter, then carefully lower into the oil. Fry in batches of two or three until golden, reheating the oil between batches, then drain on kitchen paper for 1–2 minutes.

Serve with some vanilla ice cream and a good dollop of shame and self-loathing, as befits eating a deep-fried Mars bar.

CHAPTER 7

Food to eat while you're falling in love

In which I relate how despite one
of the most GROTESQUE FIRST DATES
ever, Himself and I managed to fall in love
and so began a beautiful relationship of
COMPETITIVE EATING and bickering
over whether *Con Air* or whatever shit film
he argues in favour of is better.

It's *Con Air*, clearly.

THE STORY OF HOW I ENDED UP KISSING HIMSELF IS ONE OF THOSE EPIC TALES of near misses. A series of blunders only two people as unsuave as us could accomplish. I fully credit Jenga for my getting any action whatsoever that fateful night.

About a year before the transformative kiss that was to seal our fate, I was working in a restaurant in Dublin while I pursued my degree and flogged the dead horse of a relationship with my secondary-school boyfriend. I had this slightly unfathomable commitment to perpetuating this teenage relationship, which was, quite honestly, against his will. Essentially I forced us to stay together and effectively missed all opportunity for heady college philandering.

While at work one night, I was introduced to the 'new guy' during one shift and remember thinking quite dispassionately that he was incredibly good looking. Perhaps the only man I'd ever met who, to my mind, matched the hotness of Fox Mulder. Within the hour I had also privately nicknamed him Chris the Sheep, after a slightly gormless *Father Ted* character (who was indeed a sheep). I thought at the time that he was beautiful but probably not very intellectual. I was indeed a wanker, I know. I dismissed him outright as a romantic possibility, in part because of the dead horse relationship and in part because I didn't really give Himself a whole lot of credit. I invented a persona for Himself based on the brief conversations over staff dinner at work. I decided that he was probably a stoner who sat around playing Nintendo all day under the watchful gaze of a Bob Marley poster. In fairness to me, though, I wasn't far wrong.

A few months after that I went to Athens Art College to study for a term and it was during this time that my dead horse relationship finally gave up the ghost. The boyfriend ended it, probably doing us both a favour, though at the time I was outraged. The break-up took place on a public pay phone – a call that I had paid for. I was incensed and then I was just pretty sad. Then I ate a lot of cake and watched a lot of films from the Sandra Bullock *oeuvre*. It was all pretty textbook heartbreak stuff. I returned to Dublin, lean with despair and ready for a rebound.

In a pretty calculating way I set my sights on Himself. I decided that he was perfect rebound fodder, being both very beautiful and not a realistic relationship prospect. Actually finding Himself, however, proved tricky. It was the pre-Facebook era. I didn't know where he lived and he had left the restaurant where we met. Finally, I ran into our old manager who told me where Himself was now working, a new pizza place in town. I rallied the Bitch Herd and began to meticulously plot a casual run-in. The scheme was to go there for a boozy lunch and then take him by force if necessary.

Funnily enough, the plan never came to fruition, because a week before the appointed day, I just ran in to him by accident at a gig. I was woefully unprepared for the encounter, having been dragged virtually against my will to watch this band performing in the pouring rain. Naturally, at the exact moment of our serendipitous meeting I was wearing a bin liner.

Bin liner be damned, I still went for it. I did my best flirting impression and asked him what he was doing afterwards. He was going to another gig that night at Radio City. 'Oh, me, too,' I interjected, 'I love the Redneck Manifesto.' I'd never heard of them. 'Maybe I'll see you there.' I then made what I hoped was a sexy (though swishy), bin liner-clad exit to go find Jenga.

'We have to go to Radio City,' I shouted when I found her under her own bin liner. 'No, we have to go to Gary's house party,' she returned. That night she was also vadge-stalking some guy and, as I had come along in the role of wing-woman, I couldn't abandon her. Irritated, I agreed to go to Gary's party. Upon arriving we discovered it was one of the saddest house parties of all time. We were sitting glumly at the kitchen table when a guy walked in and said in a very bored voice, 'Uh, does anyone want these tickets to Radio City?' It was a sign, I leaped on the tickets and dragged Jenga off to get the last bus.

We had a few more false starts along the way, natch. First, I actually managed to lose the tickets before we even got there. Then, later, after successfully blagging our way past the bouncer and even managing to kiss Himself I gave him the wrong phone number, which further derailed the one-night stand we were supposed to be having. Finally, after about a week of silence on his end, I defied all Bitch Herd advice and called him. He was delighted to hear from me as he had been texting the wrong person all weekend and getting no reply. We arranged to meet for a drink in town the next day.

Our first date was an unmitigated disaster. We had two drinks in town and then Himself, clearly despairing of pub prices, and with that characteristic flair for romance that I now know and love, said, 'Do you want to get some cans and go back to mine?' Which we duly did.

Things were going reasonably well until a bit of passionate shifting, coupled with two pints and a can of Dutch Gold, most unfortunately led to me getting sick, right there in front of him. To this day it's one of the most embarrassing things ever to happen to me – and I've done a cough test, eight months pregnant, in a room full of medical students. I immediately fled.

Himself came after me and then and there asked me to be his girlfriend. None of my plan was going to plan. I was not looking for a boyfriend. I felt so mortified that I kind of never wanted to see him again, but I was also really caught up in him, even though the notion I had about him was largely true. He didn't have a Bob Marley poster, but a psychedelic Jimi Hendrix poster watched over the Nintendo. He also had a purple tie-dyed marijuana leaf wall hanging that would have to go. But I was already absolutely mad about him. He was funny and awkward, yet self-assured. And I also think that love is a bit chemical. Explaining why you loved someone from the first kiss is futile, especially as that answer changes so much over the course of a lifetime.

That first night I loved him because he was, to me, the most exciting person I'd ever met. Since then I love him because he's bitchy, he's generous, he's funny, he's completely confident, he's kind, he's arrogant as fuck, his brown eyes are my baby's brown eyes and because he is my home in this world. Also, he loves Con Air in a completely sincere, not remotely ironic way, just as much as I do.

'Loved up' is a phrase sometimes used to describe those in the first flush of love. Basically, it's that heady period of time between the first kiss and the first use of the toilet without closing the door. That initial unmuffled flush of the toilet is the death knell of loved-upness.

Those early days were a time when we tolerated each other's little foibles and idiosyncrasies. Back then, I would gladly listen to bands with names like And You Will Know Us By Our Trail Of Dead, just to share in his love of stoner metal. I would convince myself that I didn't mind his perplexing devotion to brown corduroy trousers or the fact that he possessed only three pairs of boxers. I remember them vividly, as each pair was themed: Pink Floyd, SpongeBob SquarePants and Family Guy.

I pretended his lack of interest in clothes was refreshing, even though I can imagine what went through my parents' heads the time they first met him when they encountered a sweaty, hairy six-footer wearing a T-shirt that said 'Mr Beast', who was introduced as their only child's new boyfriend. 'Hi, I'm here to violate your daughter,' it screamed.

I even tolerated a concoction of his that I later dubbed a 'hell omelette'. A grotesque, browny-grey omelette where no decisions as to what fillings actually go together were made, leading to such unlikely combinations as the salmon, goat's cheese, jalapeño and onion hell omelette. I happily tucked into such monstrosities, and many more, in the name of infatuation.

Likewise, Himself indulged me in all of my whims. He tolerated my thumb-sucking and penchant for nautical-themed outfits without complaint – things he is only too willing to mock me for now that he's got me in matrimonial lockdown.

It was in those early, loved-up days that Himself would actually consent to eating salad. I would make a salad for dinner, most likely to give the impression that I was a dainty creature with a birdlike appetite, whose favourite food was not cheese melted on Bird's Eye potato waffles with Worcestershire sauce.

In my experience, a relationship's timeline can usually be mapped quite accurately by analysing the couple's dinner plans. In the first three months, for example, very little eating occurs, as the couple is largely housebound and not inclined to fetching supplies.

Phase two (three to six months) is characterised by the casual dinner date. This is when the couple takes their love-show on the road to flaunt before all the other poor schmos trapped in phase five – the 'break up and I die alone or marry this person and wish I were dead phase' (three years to eternity). The couple looks upon the phase fivers with smug pity, safe in the knowledge that they will never sit silently in a restaurant with nothing to say to each other. They duck their heads conspiratorially and say, 'If we ever get like that … ', while eating chicken wings with cutlery. Phase three (six to 12 months) is the era of the box set and the takeaway. This couple is easily spotted as they dart from the car to the Thai place in pyjamas, carrying sweets and popcorn and about an extra stone in weight. They may be larger but they're still loved up and not to be confused with the 'since the kids we've totally let ourselves go' phase.

These days, we consume our meals in silence, unburdened by any need to appear loving, animated or even remotely interested in each other – ah, the joys of phase six: marriage.

THAI CHICKEN CURRY

During our decade-long romance curry has played an enormous role in keeping us together. I wish it was something more traditionally romantic, like strawberries and cream or a love of oysters, but, no, it's the curry obsession. It's even fed into our competitive natures, with each of us trying to outdo the other's tolerance for spice. Since I surpassed him some years ago he's been trying to claim that I've damaged my tastebuds permanently with my devotion to chillies, but I know these are the words of a pussy.

Disclaimer: These curry recipes are not claiming to be in any way authentic, they are just the dinners that we find ourselves returning to week after week because they are delicious and they don't require monumental effort or expertise. **Serves 4**

- 2 large onions, peeled and quartered
- sunflower oil, for cooking
- ½ garlic bulb, drizzled with oil
- 1 red chilli, sliced (discard the seeds if you don't want too much heat)
- 5cm piece of fresh ginger, grated
- 12 kaffir lime leaves
- 400ml coconut milk
- 2 tablespoons Thai fish sauce
- 2 skinless chicken breasts, sliced
- 1 aubergine, chopped
- 1 red pepper, deseeded and sliced
- handful of fresh coriander, chopped
- salt and freshly ground black pepper
- steamed rice and a handful of peanuts, crushed, to serve

Preheat the oven to 180°C/Gas 4. Place the onions in a roasting tin, season with salt and pepper and toss with a few tablespoons of oil. Wrap the garlic in foil, place in the tin and roast in the preheated oven for about 40 minutes, or until the onions are soft.

Heat 1 tablespoon of oil in a large saucepan over a medium heat and add the chilli, ginger and 8 lime leaves. Stir for 1–2 minutes to release the flavours, then add the roasted onions. Squeeze the garlic cloves out of their skins and add them to the pan. Cook for about 5 minutes, stirring to prevent sticking. Add the coconut milk and bring to the boil. Remove from the heat (do not remove the lime leaves), blend with a hand-held blender, then stir in the fish sauce.

Heat some oil in a frying pan, add the chicken and the remaining lime leaves and season to taste with salt and pepper. Fry until the chicken is cooked through. Add the aubergine and red pepper towards the end of cooking and cook until tender.

Remove the whole lime leaves, then add the chicken mixture to the blended sauce, along with the coriander, and simmer until heated through.

Serve with steamed rice, sprinkled with the crushed peanuts.

CHICKEN KORMA

This milder staple of the Indian takeaway has become a real fave since Himself has become such a pussy and also since Yer Man now eats dinner with us. The baby has a pretty good palate but I'm pretty sure child services would be called if we served him chilli. **Serves 2 and a toddler**

- 1 tablespoon sunflower oil
- 2 red onions, peeled and diced
- pinch of salt
- 3 skinless chicken breasts, cut into bite-sized pieces
- 3 garlic cloves, peeled and sliced
- 5-cm piece of fresh ginger, peeled and thinly sliced
- 1 tablespoon ground coriander
- 1 tablespoon ground cumin
- 1 teaspoon turmeric
- ½ teaspoon chilli powder
- 1 teaspoon ground cardamom (or the crushed seeds of about 10 pods)
- 5 cloves
- 4 tablespoons water
- 6 tablespoons ground almonds
- 300ml chicken stock
- 4 teaspoons sugar
- 4 tablespoons natural yogurt
- 4 generous tablespoons flaked almonds, toasted
- cooked rice, to serve

Heat the oil in a non-stick frying pan over a medium–high heat and add the onions and salt. Add the chicken, garlic and ginger and cook for about 5–10 minutes until the chicken is browned all over, then add the coriander, cumin, turmeric, chilli powder and cardamom.

Pinch the round tops off the cloves and add to the pan. Stir together to ensure that everything is evenly coated, adding the water to make a paste. Stir in the ground almonds, add the stock and bring to the boil, then reduce to a simmer. Simmer for about 15 minutes, or until thickened.

Remove from the heat and stir in the sugar. Stir in the yogurt just before serving, reheating gently if required, but don't allow it to boil as this will split the yogurt. Serve with cooked rice and a scattering of toasted almonds.

CHEAT ONION BHAJIS
Makes 8

- 60g oats
- 1 teaspoon turmeric
- 1 teaspoon fennel seeds
- 1 teaspoon cumin seeds
- pinch of dried chilli flakes
- ½ teaspoon salt
- 2 egg whites
- about 2 tablespoons water
- ½ large white onion, finely sliced
  into half moons
- cooking spray, for frying
- 4 tablespoons raita (see page 128),
  to serve
- chopped fresh coriander, to serve

Preheat the oven to 180°C/Gas 4. Line a baking tray with greaseproof paper. Put the oats, turmeric, fennel seeds, cumin seeds, chilli flakes and salt into a blender and blitz until the oats are finely ground. Add the egg whites and the water and blend to combine. Pour the batter into a bowl. Add the onion and toss until well coated.

Coat a non-stick frying pan with cooking spray and heat over a high heat. Using a fork, pick up quantities of the onion mixture and place on the frying pan, flattening each pile to a thickness no greater than 1 cm. Cook in two batches of four bhajis each.

Fry for about 3–5 minutes on each side, then place on the prepared baking tray and bake in the preheated oven for 5–10 minutes until crisp and completely firm. Serve with the raita and fresh coriander.

Chicken Korma, Cheat Onion Bhajis, Raita and Cheat Peshwari Naan

RAITA
Serves 2–4 as a side

- *150g natural yogurt*
- *½ cucumber, deseeded and grated*
- *large handful of mint leaves, chopped*
- *large pinch of salt*

Wrap the grated cucumber in a tea towel and squeeze out any excess water. Combine the cucumber with the remaining ingredients and serve.

CHEAT PESHWARI NAAN

To my mind so much of delicious Indian cooking is about the gorgeous sides, hence my preoccupation with bhajis and raita. As no Indian meal is complete without a naan or the delightfully named poppadom, Himself and I usually make these cheat naan pittas that are slightly easier to make at home. **Serves 2**

- *20g sultanas*
- *20g desiccated coconut*
- *20g flaked almonds*
- *1 tablespoon butter*
- *2 pitta breads*

Preheat the oven to 180°C/Gas 4. Combine the sultanas, coconut, almonds and butter and stuff the mixture into the pitta breads. Place on a baking tray and bake in the preheated oven for about 5 minutes, or until slightly crispy.

n

u

CHAPTER 8

Drugs are f

In which I sample the many delights of both NATURAL AND CHEMICAL HIGHS. Unsurprisingly this chapter features several fried sandwiches.

OTHER PEOPLE'S DRUG STORIES ARE USUALLY PRETTY BORING, SO I'LL TRY to keep mine brief and informative, at the very least. I don't really remember the first time I smoked a joint, but I have a kind of composite image in my head that goes something like this:

It is after school at the DART station, and I'm probably around 14 or 15 years old. We're huddled together in the kind of all-pervading drizzle that actually makes one wetter than full-tilt rain. As is the case with all school-issued garments that come in contact with moisture of any kind, the navy wool jumpers that everyone is wearing give off the smell of wet dog. This odour is mingling with the intriguing, oily, earthy smell of what is most likely fairly crap Dublin hash. The cool guys, Owen and Simon, are passing around what looks like a really feeble cigarette, admonishing everyone for 'duck-arseing'. I don't really know what they mean by this, but then I am hopelessly naïve and unworldly. I blame this on my lack of older siblings. I possess zero street smarts and must rely on my knowledgeable, cool girlfriend Jen, who routinely saves me from embarrassing social blunders. She grew up on the mean streets of South County Dublin, and I idolise her as much as I am hopelessly jealous of her. I smoke the joint when it's handed to me, and I don't sputter or cough as in an American coming-of-age movie. I just have a few drags and pass it on. We all get giggly for a few minutes, and I emulate what I imagine a high person to be. Then my friend Mark (who is one of those six-foot 14-year-olds who literally has no clue what to be doing with his giant man-body) goes green and has to kneel down with his head almost touching the ground. Seeing Mark felled by a skinny, crooked little joint is somehow hilarious. Jen and I are dispatched to get him a sandwich from the shop up near school by Owen and Simon, who are experienced in such matters and know what Mark needs. After a few bites, Mark looks better. The DART comes and I go home, where I eat red Cheddar cheese melted on a pitta and congratulate myself on not doing anything stupid in front of Owen and Simon.

So it was a pretty ho-hum introduction to getting stoned. My first foray into drugs didn't produce a sudden insatiable appetite for crystal meth, as threatened by the 'don't do drugs' seminars that we occasionally had in school. I just had a pretty take-it-or-leave-it attitude about hash for most of my teens. And I was certainly never enamoured of it enough to procure my own supply at any stage. In my group of friends there was no pressure to partake. Some did, some didn't and some bought their own. The ones who bought their own were very generous about sharing – I think generally they just wanted the company. So it was a fairly average adolescence of getting binned on Friday nights in the park or in Dave's shed, and then ambling home spritzing perfume and trying not to act overly suspicious. I always wonder what I'll do when my son, Yer Man, starts arriving home with a studied nonchalance, reeking of Lynx. Probably show him *Requiem for a Dream* immediately.

To be totally honest, I didn't see getting stoned as that much of an issue. I got good marks in school, and I was very committed to getting into art college. I saw classmates getting wrecked at 11.00 break and thought 'well, I'm not that bad'. Of course, it was this kind of thinking that led me to psychiatric care at a later stage. Oops.

At the time, I don't remember mental health as a topic that was on the agenda all that much. I was deeply, embarrassingly, almost stagily angsty as a teenager and was always crying and moodily listening to Fiona Apple and reading about Sylvia Plath. Fortunately, I had a group of friends with a low tolerance for my histrionics. And I think slash hope that I have to some extent grown out of this by now.

One friend did attempt suicide in our late teens, and I remember a gang of us cleaning up after he had gone to hospital. It was a sobering moment, but I honestly didn't see any connection between cleaning up my friend's blood and his drinking and smoking spliffs every day. I don't know whether he would reach any conclusions based on this either and it's really not for me to say, one way or another. It was just another one of those days in the series of chaotic days that make up being a teenager. It's just a batshit crazy time, figuring out who you are, alongside everyone else figuring out who they are.

I now look at my younger relatives who are leaving school and starting college, and I think they seem so incredibly savvy. They bear no resemblance whatsoever to my teenage self. They're eating healthily and going on yoga retreats, and they look incredibly groomed. They have blogs with paid advertising and product endorsements. They baffle me. At their age, I still hadn't mastered matching the colour of my foundation to the colour of my face.

In my second year of college, I got my first taste of how utterly brilliant drugs can be. Don't be mad at me for saying that. Part of the problem with drugs education as I see it, is that the message 'Drugs are bad' ignores the fact that the most seductive element of drugs is that they are sometimes so very good. The message leaves no room for nuance. It's too definitive. 'Drugs are bad.' This leads to someone trying drugs, finding that they don't immediately die or end up in prostitution and then leaves them distrustful of the message as a whole. I know, because this is what happened to me. I took drugs, had a brilliant time, and I distinctly remember thinking (rather stupidly), 'These drugs aren't bad, these drugs are brilliant.' Cut to St John of Gods three years later and yeah, maybe they weren't so brilliant.

The first time I did magic mushrooms was one of the most memorable, incredible, delightful nights of my life. I know, I know. That statement isn't exactly 'on message', but I'm hoping the over-riding image of me on Olanzapine some years later will remind you that I paid dearly for those few hours of bliss.

I was camping with friends at the edge of a forest when some mushroom tea was produced, along with curious tiny little mushrooms that had the look and texture of hazelnuts. I felt some trepidation but decided to give them a go.

That first trip was like a montage of drug trip clichés. I cried because the stars 'were so beautiful'. I took my shoes off and skipped through the enchanted forest that glowed in the darkness. At one point, I actually hugged a tree. In fact, I spent a really long time hugging that tree. I sat cross-legged beside it, with my arm slung around its trunk like we were old pals. I was watching my other arm, which was turning into liquid and pooling into a vast lake in my lap. So, ya know, I was pretty fucking high. The trip kind of concluded with a luxurious nap on my friend's belly. It was such a cosy and bizarre ending. Just as the lap lake had seemed so huge and expansive and yet at the same time had fit snugly into my lap, her belly was like a cosy little warm pillow, but also, at the same time, seemed to stretch away from me into infinity.

Tripping is pretty trippy. That warped perception of size and space is something that has stayed with me ever since. When I was brainsick and quite mad it took on a very sinister tinge; I call it the infinity feeling. It's quite hard to describe but it goes something like this: I close my eyes and the space behind my eyes seems to stretch and grow and distort until it feels infinite and somehow a bit terrifying.

Lots of my drug-induced behaviour was pretty much what you'd imagine it was like. It was all pretty standard and disappointingly banal for the most part. I flew a kite through a field barefoot at dawn, I had long, largely senseless conversations on esoteric topics like 'infinity as a concept: discuss', and 'what is your favourite biscuit?' with similarly incoherent beings sitting at the bottom of the stairs at house parties. I accidentally smashed the top of a bottle of absinthe and, unperturbed, proceeded to drink the absinthe through the cardigan I was wearing as a precaution. I encountered my roommate and asked him what day it was. He misheard me and told me the date (4 May). I platonically slept with people. I platonically wrestled people. I danced really, really badly. A lot. I told a DJ that his set reminded me of a lunar landing. That kind of shite.

Cooking, it has to be said, didn't figure hugely in my life at this point. It being art college, at least one of my friends was dabbling in veganism, and there was a helluva lot of hummus kicking around at this stage. We started college in Thomas Street the same year that paninis arrived in Dublin. It was also the dawn of the latte era. Being thoroughly middle-class art students who had never gone further than Christchurch Cathedral, we wanted to integrate, so we frequented the local pubs and eateries. In the local Chinese someone (probably one of the vegans) foolishly ordered a salad, which was duly produced, deep fried, in a paper bag. Even more disturbing, we heard that someone was shot in the face in one of the pubs we students had adopted. That was quite enough integrating. We retreated back inside the college for the most part and ate our hummus and drank our lattes.

FRIED PEANUT BUTTER SANDWICH

Being either stoned, high or hungover for a large part of my college years, coupled with the influence of the newly imported panini, led to my consuming a lot of fried sandwiches during this time. Any readers of my column will know about my abiding love of the fried sandwich. Indeed, anyone who's seen me in swimming togs can probably attest to this love also. Fried sandwiches, in my experience, don't go straight to your hips or even your stomach. In fact, they create a new outpost of fat under your ass cheeks, thus giving the appearance of a double ass. The best thing about the fried sandwich as a meal concept is that it can work as breakfast, lunch, dinner or dessert. Heart attack-inducing and so versatile ...

This was famously an Elvis fave. Not sure if that's much of a recommendation ...

Serves 1 (best enjoyed alone, as others will judge you for it)

- 2 teaspoons butter
- 2 slices white bread
- 2 tablespoons peanut butter
- ½ teaspoon ground cinnamon
- ½ banana, thinly sliced
- 1 teaspoon clear honey

Spread the butter on one side of both slices of bread. Then spread the unbuttered side of one of the slices with the peanut butter, sprinkle with the cinnamon, top with the banana and drizzle with the honey. Place the remaining slice of bread on top, buttered side up.

Heat a non-stick frying pan over a medium–high heat. Add the sandwich to the pan and cook for a few minutes on each side until it is golden and crunchy.

PAN-FRIED BACON AND BRIE SANDWICH WITH APRICOT JAM

For many years, Himself's nights out were plagued by bad luck. He was always getting a 'bad pint' or an 'iffy curry chips' and could usually be found spooning a toilet before dawn.

For a brief time, we had a bedroom that had a cast-iron, free-standing bathtub beside the bed. I had visions of enjoying a Cadbury's Flake in it, while sheet music swirled to the floor around me, until Himself, after nights out, began to treat the bath as a remote toilet. I couldn't even look at it without images of something that looked like mango chutney and smelled like badness flashing across my brain.

In our current home, the bathtub is downstairs, and I dared to hope that this inconvenience might cure Himself of his predilection for tub-spewing. I figured that we are parents now, and that defiling bathtubs was a thing of the past.

However, not long after Yer Man was born, I was proved wrong. I woke in the night to that old familiar sound of the 'bad pint' being regurgitated. I was aware that the sounds were disturbingly close, but I was too tired to take action and went back to sleep. In the morning, however, I uncovered a depraved scene. Himself was curled, foetus-like, around the baby bath. Even more horrific was the fact that he hadn't even bothered to put in the stopper, and some kind of hell juice was slowly draining out onto the floor.

My first instinct was to launch a reign of intense passive-aggression, manifesting as prolonged silent treatment, during which I would do housework really loudly. But I pulled back and realised that the best course of action was mercy. That is how this sandwich came to be ...

It can really only be attempted when you are so filled with self-loathing and remorse that eating a fried cheese-and-bacon sandwich doesn't seem so bad when compared with your original crimes. **Serves 1**

- 2 tablespoons butter (don't skip this bit, as it is the main source of the cure)
- 2 slices thick white bread (I think sourdough is the nicest, rather than sliced pan)
- 2 crispy bacon rashers
- 4 slices Brie
- 1 tablespoon apricot jam

Preheat the oven to 150°C/Gas 2. Put about 1 tablespoon of the butter in an ovenproof cast-iron frying pan over a medium–high heat and heat until melted. Put a slice of bread on the pan and then top it with the bacon and cheese.

Spread the jam on one side of the other slice of bread and place this, jam-side down, on top of the bread in the pan. Spread the top of this slice with the remaining butter. When the underside of the sandwich is golden brown, flip it, then put the pan in the preheated oven for about 5 minutes to finish.

PULLED PORK WITH ASIAN PICKLE

Pickle and pulled pork is just the kind of tasty, supremely savoury fare that the stoner in me will always yearn for, and I am passionately devoted to this slow-cooked version, good stuffed into a soft roll, served over rice or, more often than not, just plucked straight from the pot and shoved into my mouth. **Serves 4**

- 2.5-cm piece of fresh ginger, peeled
  and roughly chopped
- 1 onion, peeled
- 2 garlic cloves, peeled
- 1 tablespoon olive oil
- 2 teaspoons chilli powder
- 1 teaspoon ground cumin
- ½ teaspoon ground cinnamon
- 1 teaspoon Chinese five-spice
  powder
- 600ml chicken stock
- 3 tablespoons tomato ketchup
- 3 tablespoons soy sauce
- 3 tablespoons clear honey
- 4 whole star anise
- 4 bay leaves
- 1 pork loin fillet, about 450g, cut
  into 4 pieces
- salt and freshly ground black pepper
- cooked rice, or 4 soft bread rolls,
  to serve

Asian pickle
- 200ml rice wine vinegar
- 200ml water
- 100g sugar
- 1 tablespoon salt
- 1 cucumber, thinly sliced
- ½ red onion, thinly sliced

Place the ginger, onion and garlic in a food processor and blitz for a couple of seconds.

Heat the oil in a heavy-based saucepan, add the ginger, onion and garlic mixture, along with a pinch of salt and some pepper, the chilli powder, cumin, cinnamon and five-spice powder. Stir over the heat for a few minutes to soften the onion and incorporate the spices.

Add the stock, ketchup, soy sauce and honey to the pan and stir. When the liquid is simmering, add the star anise, bay leaves and pork pieces. Cover and simmer for 40 minutes–1 hour; if the liquid doesn't quite cover the meat, just turn the meat a few times during the cooking.

Meanwhile, to make the Asian pickle, combine the vinegar, water, sugar and salt in a bowl, stirring to dissolve the sugar, then add the cucumber and onion.

The pork is ready when it is tender and pulls apart easily, and the sauce is reduced and thickened. Using two forks, shred the pork and serve it on a bed of rice or in a warm bread roll, whichever you're using, with the sauce spooned over it, topped with the Asian pickle.

CHAPTER 9

Drugs are the worst

In which drugs TURN ON ME
SPECTACULARLY and I don't have
appetite for much of anything.

THE FIRST EXPERIENCE I EVER HAD OF A BAD TRIP WAS IN MY FINAL YEAR OF college. I had just handed in my thesis and had gone to Amsterdam with Himself in celebration. I still absolutely love Amsterdam, even though my initial enthusiasm for the place has shifted into slightly less psychedelic realms. But back then we were basically going on a trip to have a trip. At that point Himself and I had never done mushrooms together save for a failed 'shroom-picking camping trip in Wicklow that saw us each eating a huge plate of slimy, slug-like Liberty Bells that had no effect on us whatsoever. We went on a night-time hike through a sodden, drizzly forest clutching a bottle of Buckfast in an attempt to 'activate' the mushies. When this didn't produce any hallucinations we retreated back to the tent, which had unfortunately collapsed in our absence.

In Amsterdam, we had booked into a tiny attic room in a little hotel. The room was at the top of some vertigo-inducing stairs that would later pose problems when we attempted to exit the room while high off our heads.

We bought our mushrooms from a head shop around the corner and skipped back to the room like giddy kids. About 20 minutes after eating the mushrooms, Himself started complaining that the mushrooms were duds and that nothing was happening. He started pacing, muttering about going back to the shop. I, meanwhile, was barely capable of speech as I stared at the painting on the wall behind him, which was suddenly and vividly exploding to life.

In the painting was a sailing boat with rockets attached to the hull – though I suspect this addition was made by me rather than the artist. As Himself whined on, I watched as the boat blasted off from the painting and began making its way up into the Earth's atmosphere. My focus returned briefly to Himself, long enough to form the thought: 'What is he talking about, these mushies are crazy!' He weighed about four stone more than me and so presumably was slower on the up than I was.

About an hour later we were playing with the taps in the bathroom with completely disproportionate delight, 20 minutes after that we were rolling on the floor, 'swimming', as you do, and soon after that we became completely engrossed in a pop-up book called *The Universe*. The book was a childhood favourite of Himself's and featured pop-up depictions of things like the Big Bang and the death of a star. 'Ooooooooooohhhhhh! Aaaaaaaaaaahhhhhhhh!' we exclaimed with each turn of the page. After a while, the book was getting to be a bit much for our sparking, popping, mushie-addled brains, and by mutual consent we put it away.

Describing a trip is so difficult, and I presume that it's different for different people. The thing I always found with magic mushrooms was that the drugs have a way of ebbing and flowing. All your thoughts and sensations have a way of winding up tighter and tighter and then suddenly spiralling out in this incredibly pleasurable release. Everything is colourful and beautiful – even just breathing is pretty fun while on mushrooms.

What I always loved so much about it was the way one's senses would kind of pull a switcheroo. In the throes of a trip I have chewed on colours and tasted songs and marvelled at how time suddenly seems like a physical thing and the spaces around you become both tiny and yet boundless all at the same time. Basically it's a head fuck. When it's going well it's a brilliant head fuck, but when it goes badly it is a nightmare.

So back to the room. The next thing I remember was that we were suddenly in my parents' bedroom and, even more disturbing, that we WERE my parents. 'For fuck's sake,' I said, 'why am I my dad? For fuck's sake.' I couldn't seem to snap back out of this level of the hallucination. I found I'd started to repeat 'For fuck's sake, for fuck's sake', over and over. Or maybe I was just thinking it. Either way I couldn't stop saying it and suddenly I felt quite certain that I would never stop saying it. 'For fuck's sake, for fuck's sake.' I was stuck in a loop, like the needle of a record-player getting stuck in a groove.

The more I tried to stop thinking, the more the phrase repeated itself. It felt like I was in that other room, my mind stuttering away for anywhere between two minutes and six hours. When I finally snapped back from my freaky parents' bedroom and the relentless loop of 'for fuck's sake', I was relieved to find that the mushrooms were easing off somewhat. We smoked a joint, which gave everything a distinctly cosier feeling, then we decided to bundle up and join the other legions of stoned tourists walking the streets of Amsterdam in the snow.

That may not seem like the worst trip ever but it was enough to scare me off mushrooms for good. I didn't like the strange, looping thoughts and the way what had been fun and full of delight a few minutes before had flipped quite suddenly into something surreal and menacing. It also gave me a sense that my brain wasn't up to the neurological gymnastics of hallucinogenics any more. I sensibly backed off on the mushrooms, but not so sensibly continued to smoke weed and upped my Ecstasy intake in place of the 'shrooms, because, you've guessed it, I am a genius.

I was in my final year of college and – despite how it sounds – I was actually very committed to doing well. I didn't remotely think of myself as a druggie type person. I just thought of myself as someone who enjoyed a spliff before dinner in the evening and before breakfast on the weekend. As I said before, I was surrounded by people who were far worse than me and seemed pretty high functioning. Or maybe just pretty high.

Around this time there was a penchant for legal highs among some of our friends. Labs were producing drugs that imitated the effects of speed and Ecstasy with chemicals that had not yet been declared controlled substances. These were way handier to procure than ordinary pills and we sampled them enthusiastically. Being high on pills was way different from mushrooms and not nearly as fun to my mind. I didn't take pills very often. Certainly not every weekend, but more for special occasions, like a gig where Himself and I were officially the highest and least popular members of the audience, arriving as we did in home-made rabbit costumes that stank as we sweated and moshed around in them, shedding polyester fur all over the people unfortunate enough to be standing in our vicinity.

I finished my degree that summer and started to work in a second-hand bookshop. Himself and I were living in the old, ivy-covered stone coach house down the bottom of his dad's garden. The coach house was cold and damp, with a rickety ladder up to the bedroom under the eaves. It was more like a treehouse than a cottage and we loved it. There were apple trees in the garden and a cast-iron claw-footed bathtub in the bedroom beside the bed, which was a favourite spot for a soggy spliff and a glass of wine.

We made plans to go travelling with friends in the autumn. We bought the plane tickets that would take us across three continents over the course of a year. I mulled over doing an MA afterwards or moving to London to work in a gallery. I was 22 and I didn't have any concrete notion about what my life would become. I had been included in a few exhibitions off the back of my degree show in NCAD and was even mentioned by name in the *Irish Times* write-up, but I was feeling a bit ambivalent towards art after four years of study.

This is about the time that I took my last ever pill at Electric Picnic 2007. As I said in the opening chapter, I was enjoying a night like any other at that time. I was in the back of a huge tent when I began to feel the pill taking effect. My toes and then my feet started to feel very warm, then the tingling sensation continued on up my legs. I was relaxed and happy, enjoying the music and the pleasant sensation of seratonin and dopamine crackling and fizzing across my brain.

Then I felt an odd sensation that was a bit like that moment when you're standing in the sea and a wave passes and lifts you up briefly. These 'waves' started coming with more and more frequency. I left my friends in the tent and went outside to get some air. I was starting to feel quite panicky and the wave sensations were becoming stronger, and with them came a feeling of blackest dread. Suddenly I was absolutely petrified. Festival-goers swarmed everywhere around me, but I had no idea where my friends were. The more I tried to calm myself the more wound up and scared I became. It felt like my brain was turning on me and I have never felt so exposed and vulnerable and abjectly frightened. This might sound a bit dramatic, but I felt that I was going to die.

I don't know why I didn't just go to the first aid tent. I wish I had, obviously. They might've given me something to calm me down, but instead I went back to my tent. I don't even know how I got there in my frantic state but I did. I lay in the tent trying to ride out the terrifying sensations. I was racked with waves of panic. I lay on my side with my fists clenched, my eyes shut, my face frozen in a twisted grimace. I felt like my brain was in spasm, and the hours passed with virtually no let-up in the roaring terror. During random moments of clarity I wondered how much more of this could I take. I imagined my brain shorting, like a light going out, and someone finding my body hours later.

I made it to morning and felt a bit more normal. There was still something off, though. I was scared, the morning light looked murky and there was a low buzzing sound, the source of which I could not locate until I realised it was just in my head. I smiled at my friends and tried to act normal. I heard myself tell them I'd fallen asleep in my tent early and I got the first inkling of what was to become an almost constant sense of surreal detachment from myself and those around me. For the first time, I was suddenly conscious of seeing the world through a pair of eyes. It was like in movies when a character looks through binoculars and the scene is framed by funny black circles. It was as if life was taking place at a remove all of a sudden. Oh God, I was feeling pretty weird.

I tried to calm myself down as we drove back to Dublin. We got stuck in traffic and I had a mad urge to flee the car for no reason whatsoever. Himself and a friend were sitting in the front seat playing music and dissecting the events of the weekend. Despite having joined me in the tent some time near dawn, I'm pretty sure Himself hadn't picked up on anything strange. In the back seat I was doing my best to rationalise the situation in my head. 'You had a bad experience but the drug is out of your system. You just need a good night's sleep. We'll get home and have a camomile tea and watch a movie. It's all fine now.'

Over and over I repeated the mantra 'you're fine, it's over, the mean drugs are gone, you're safe now', all the way back to Dublin. We got to our house and I did feel a bit more normal. Later, we walked to the Thai place to get noodles and I felt giddy at feeling better. Then I felt it, that unmistakable 'wave' travelling up my legs, lifting me briefly and filling me again with the most indescribable, blackest panic. The fear seemed to literally pour into my body. It suddenly felt exactly like I was coming up on a pill again just like the night before, only I hadn't taken anything in more than 24 hours. Something was very wrong.

ULTIMATE CRUMBLE

Chapters about drug-taking in a cookbook don't exactly lend themselves to the whole recipe theme we're supposed to be adhering to, and I have to admit that eating and cooking were not my biggest focus during this time! However, Himself and I did have a few culinary favourites, though they were largely informed by being very stoned. For the purposes of propriety and the assumption that most readers are not currently very stoned I have given these dishes a bit of an update.

In the halcyon days of the coach house we made endless apple tarts from the apple trees in the garden. Being the incorrigible stoners that we were the apple tarts were then subjected to many borderline disgusting accompaniments. We often served a slice warm, topped with an entire Brunch ice cream, though we didn't stop there. Next we would sprinkle over some cereal (Crunchy Nut Cornflakes work really well) and, lastly, pour milk over the entire concoction. I'll spare you the recipe for that one. **Serves 6–8**

- 500g cooking apples, peeled, cored and chopped into 2-cm pieces
- juice of ½ lemon
- 100g granulated white sugar
- 350g frozen berries
- 110g plain flour
- 150g soft brown sugar
- 120g rolled oats

- 1 teaspoon ground ginger
- 1½ teaspoons ground cardamom
- 100g cashew nuts
- 100g desiccated coconut
- 100g pecan nuts, chopped
- 150g butter, plus 15g for greasing
- vanilla ice cream (or Brunch ice cream!), to serve

Preheat the oven to 180°C/Gas 4. Place the apples in a saucepan over a medium heat. Add the lemon juice, white sugar and frozen berries. Stir until the berries have thawed, then bring the mixture to the boil and allow it to bubble for 5 minutes. When the apples are tender, remove from the heat. Drain off about half of the liquid released from the fruit, then set the fruit aside. In a large bowl, combine the flour, brown sugar, oats, ginger, cardamom, cashew nuts, coconut and pecan nuts. Melt the butter in a saucepan over a gentle heat. Pour the melted butter over the dry ingredients and mix well with your hands.

Lightly grease a deep ovenproof dish, roughly 20cm in diameter. Pour in the apples and berries and top with the crumble mixture. Place an oven tray underneath the crumble (to catch any spillover) and bake in the middle of the preheated oven for 30–40 minutes, or until the crumble is golden brown and the fruit mixture is bubbling up at the edges. Remove from the oven and leave to stand for about 15 minutes before serving.

Serve this fragrant, delicious crumble with a good-quality vanilla ice cream, or a Brunch ice cream topped with Crunchy Nut Cornflakes if you happen to be stoned!

Ultimate Crumble

ULTIMATE CHOCOLATE BISCUIT CAKE

Stoners don't usually have the wherewithal to bake from scratch. This chocolate biscuit cake, however, was just about manageable for us in our monged state and so worth the hour and a half of bumbling and trudging around the kitchen. Cook's tip: How about skipping the spliff and just making the cake ... **Serves 12–16**

150g milk chocolate, broken into pieces

- *100g plain chocolate, broken into pieces*
- *125g butter*

75g golden syrup

- *150g digestive biscuits*
- *2 Crunchie bars*
- *100g mini marshmallows*
- *50g white chocolate, broken into pieces*

Line a 20-cm round springform cake tin with baking paper. Put the milk chocolate and the plain chocolate into a heatproof bowl set over a saucepan of gently simmering water and heat, stirring, until almost completely melted. Add the butter and golden syrup and stir until everything is melted and fully combined. Remove from the heat.

Place the digestive biscuits in a polythene bag and gently bash them with a rolling pin. Using the rolling pin, bash the Crunchies in their packets. Don't bash them too much, as you don't want to turn them into dust.

Add the crushed biscuits and Crunchies to the melted chocolate mixture in the bowl, along with the mini marshmallows, and stir well to combine. Spoon the mixture into the prepared tin, spreading it evenly and pressing it in to flatten the surface. Leave to set.

Put the white chocolate into a heatproof bowl set over a saucepan of gently simmering water and heat, stirring, until melted. Drizzle the chocolate in thin lines over the top of the cake and leave to set, then unclip and release the springform and cut the cake into 16 thin slices.

SWEETCORN, SPRING ONION AND COMTÉ CHEESE FRITTERS

These cheesy fritters are the best breakfast item I have ever had and they also do very nicely for supper. **Serves 4 (12 fritters)**

- 110g plain flour
- 1 teaspoon baking powder
- pinch of salt
- 1 tablespoon sugar
- 3 eggs
- 110ml milk
- 325g tinned sweetcorn, drained
- 3 spring onions, finely sliced
- large handful of fresh basil, finely shredded
- 100g Comté cheese, grated
- sunflower oil, for frying
- poached eggs, bacon and tomatoes, to serve

Combine the flour, baking powder, salt and sugar in a bowl and whisk in the eggs and the milk, ensuring there are no lumps of flour in the mix. Leave the batter to rest for a few minutes. Add the sweetcorn, spring onions, basil and cheese.

Heat the oil in a frying pan over a medium–high heat and spoon large dollops of batter into the pan. Cook until little bubbles appear on the top, then flip the fritters over and cook for a further 5 minutes, until golden brown and firm. You'll need to cook a few batches, adding a little more oil to the pan each time. Keep the fritters warm in the oven until ready to serve with poached eggs, bacon and tomatoes. Enjoy!

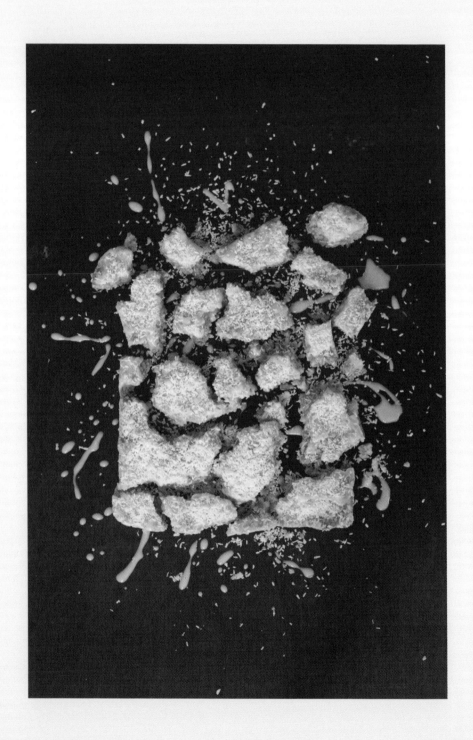

LEMON TIFFIN SQUARES

If the chocolate biscuit cake on page 156 is the ULTIMATE choccie biscuit cake recipe, then this recipe is like its delicious evil twin, the yin to its yang, almost like a refreshing palate cleanser for the baking world – if the words palate cleanser and condensed milk can in fact co-exist in a recipe. It is sharp and sweet and yum.

This recipe was given to me by Jessom, Bitch Herd co-founder and all round cooking boss. She doesn't invite me over to dinner enough. I'm just going to leave that admonishment hanging there, for what else are memoirs slash cookbooks good for except putting pressure on friends to invite me over more?

Makes 12 medium-sized squares

- *125g butter*
- *175ml tinned condensed milk*
- *250g digestive biscuits, roughly crushed*
- *100g desiccated coconut, plus extra for sprinkling*
- *zest and juice of 1½ lemons*
- *200g icing sugar, sifted*

Line a 24-cm square baking tin with baking paper. Put the butter and condensed milk in a saucepan over a medium heat and stir until the butter is melted and has combined with the milk. Put the biscuits, coconut and lemon zest into a large bowl and pour the condensed-milk-and-butter mixture over it. Mix everything together until all the dry ingredients are well coated.

Pour the mixture into the prepared tin and press it firmly into all the corners. Place in the fridge for at least 1 hour to set.

Mix the icing sugar and the lemon juice together until smooth. When the base is firm and chilled, pour the icing evenly over it and sprinkle the top with desiccated coconut. Chill in the fridge overnight, then cut the tiffin block into squares with a sharp knife.

CREAMY BEANS ON TOAST WITH CHORIZO

This is one fuck-off fancy version of beans on toast, adapted from a recipe by my former boss Maisha Lenehan, cook and owner of Bibi's Café. This dish demands to be made immediately if not sooner. I can't tell you how delicious it is. **Serves 2**

- 1 tablespoon olive oil
- ½ onion, peeled and finely sliced into half moons
- 1 garlic clove, finely sliced
- 100g chorizo sausage, peeled, halved lengthways and chopped into small cubes
- 200ml white wine
- 80g crème fraîche
- 400g tinned cannellini beans, drained and rinsed
- small bunch of fresh thyme
- pinch of dried chilli flakes (optional)
- 4 slices sourdough bread or other nice white bread, toasted
- grated Parmesan cheese, to serve

Pour the oil into a medium-sized saucepan and place it over a medium heat. Add the onion and sauté until transparent, then add the garlic and cook for a couple of minutes.

Add the chorizo to the pan. Increase the heat to allow the chorizo to release its rich oils, and stir frequently to prevent sticking.

Taste the wine to ensure quality (a glass or two will do!), then add to the pan. Bring to the boil, then reduce the heat and simmer for 5–10 minutes until the liquid has reduced by about two-thirds. Stir in the crème fraîche.

Add the beans to the pan and cook for 1 minute until heated through. Stir in the thyme and chilli flakes, if using – some people find that the chorizo adds enough of a kick to the dish. I usually skip any additional seasoning because the chorizo is generally salty enough.

Serve the bean mixture on top of the toasted bread, along with a healthy sprinkling of grated Parmesan cheese.

CHAPTER 10

Moving back in with my parents

In which I, you've guessed it,
move back in with my parents as an adult
(never a good look) and have to fend for
myself in the BARREN WASTELAND
that is their fridge. I also start to feel
gradually less mental.

AFTER I SETTLED IN TO BEING MAD, AS IF TO COMPOUND FURTHER THE ALREADY deeply depressing fact of being on anti-depressants and anti-psychotics, I then moved back in with my parents. After months of pretending I was fine to virtually everyone I knew, it came as a relief, of sorts, to just tell everyone some version of the truth and give up my (frankly exhausting) one-woman show called 'I'm completely fine! Fine, fine, fine (while internally I am losing my shit)'.

The cacophony inside my head didn't shut up all at once, but there was a certain relief to just crawling inside my sick brain and letting go of life. I let go of going travelling with my friends – that would have been an unmitigated disaster, seeing as how I could barely get myself together enough to go to the supermarket. I let go of going to work every day and quit my job in the bookshop. I let go of Himself and very, very forcefully told him to leave and go travelling without me. I let go of my independence and moved back in with my mum and dad. It sounds like a mass copping out of life, but I literally couldn't manage the most basic of things. I kept cancelling appointments with the psychiatrist and the counsellor, and even those phone calls required monumental psyching up. Basically, even the very act of copping out was too demanding for me.

I feel I should say that before I was ill, I was not a copper outer. I was lazy but not a copper outer. I was, prior to this, a pretty robust personality, so I think people found it odd that I had become somehow small and quiet in myself. I stopped taking the Olanzapine because I was struggling to function on it, and I also had a pathological fear of drugs by this stage.

I did stick with the anti-depressants as I found that I couldn't exactly detect them in my system as strongly as I did the Olanzapine. And I was also afraid of what I might do if I came off them. The intrusive thoughts that assailed me constantly around this time were that (a) I would kill myself, or (b) I would kill someone else. As I said before, the terribly irritating catch-22 of these things is that the thoughts feel like they are not your own, which makes you feel scared, very scared. And then, because the thoughts are producing a very real physical reaction, this seems somehow to back up the sense that these thoughts are powerful and real. And then, as your body responds to the perceived danger of the thoughts, it somehow causes the thoughts to become even more persistent, until it literally feels like you're thinking 'What if I murder my family tonight?' up to 30 times a minute. It's exhausting, and it's also why simple things like picking up the phone to cancel the psychiatrist seem like insurmountable difficulties. And, obviously, I hardly need to say this, but if you are thinking 'What if I murder my family tonight?' up to 30 times a minute, then cancelling the psychiatrist is quite possibly the last thing you should be doing at this point.

I think a lot of the reason why my phobic thoughts dwelled on the whole matricide thing is because my mother is a total nightmare … that's a joke. No, I think the reason for this obsessive thought was because, as it is for many people, killing my family is actually my worst nightmare. I would obsessively read stories about violent crimes and think 'is this how that person felt right before they did that awful thing?' Basically, I wondered, did I have what they have?

Part of the problem as I see it for the general population that don't have much hands-on experience of mental illness (like me back then), is that with all the labels like schizophrenia and depression and psychosis we sometimes don't realise just how nuanced a diagnosis can be.

Personally, I no longer want a diagnosis. When I think back to that time, it was the worst of my life, and labels like psychotic depression, or panic disorder or 'feeling anxious' (as my mother euphemistically called it) really didn't perk me up. For most of us our perception of those labels is that they describe permanent states. And that is how I felt back then, aged 22. I felt that I was permanently damaged. And really, thinking of our bodies or our minds as either 'fixed' or 'broken' is not good for anyone and it's not entirely accurate either.

So anyway, there I was, 'broken', thinking that my arm was possessed and that quite possibly any day now I would kill my family. I was moping around my parents' house avoiding all stimulants, eating manuka honey and drinking camomile tea. Not having a job was driving me as crazy as having a job had done, so I began to look for something to occupy myself and distract me from the 'murder thoughts'.

Around this time, I was trying to do more wholesome things, like watching *Seventh Heaven* on the sofa at my parent's house and hiking with friends at the weekends. It was during one of these outings that I fell, badly tore the ligaments in my right ankle and wound up on crutches. 'That'll give you something to talk about with Dr Den,' said Herself, apparently completely unaware that counselling is not really about catching up on one's news, exactly.

The crutches seemed like karma made manifest. They felt like a reminder that some people actually had more tangible problems instead of spending all their time worrying that their whole life up until that point was a fictional construct and that reality didn't exist.

Crutches are the worst, even just making a cup of tea and bringing it to the sofa is a logistical headache. Never mind getting oneself from job interview to job interview. Though I think the crutches helped in that I garnered a bit of sympathy and they gave the impression that I was a go-getter with a bit of gumption – 'no crutches will hold me back' – which couldn't have been further from the reality.

I ended up with a temp job in a software company, Fenvil, in Dublin's IFSC. It was my first (and pretty much last) time working in an office and I actually really liked it. It was pure novelty all day for me. Answering phones in my special 'phone' voice, wearing pencil skirts and striding around (once I'd ditched the crutches) with faux purpose. It was a good reintroduction to functioning. I had to talk to people in the office, and I also had to do stuff.

One of my biggest areas of influence in Fenvil was the tuck shop. Though it was more of a tuck filing cabinet. It was my remit to stock the tuck shop, and I also held the keys – the tuck shop had strict opening hours stipulated by the CEO, and no one could access it outside of these hours except for me. I was always fascinated that the CEO took such an interest in the tuck shop, though it started to make sense when I began receiving all manner of emails from the programmers attempting to gain admittance outside of tuck shop operating hours. I naturally abused the shit out of this and charged a fee of one Balisto bar for each illicit transaction.

The fact that I was taking an interest in and even trading in the tuck shop black market seemed like a positive sign. I was getting out of my head more. I was swimming each day before work and that hour alone with my thoughts was no longer a thought spiral of terror and anxiety. I was gradually getting better at managing the manic thinking.

I also finally came clean to Herself about what exactly had happened. It wasn't the most fun conversation ever. Admitting that everything that's happening to you is pretty much all your fault and that you've been doing drugs and possibly broken your stupid brain for good is about as much fun as the Olanzapine. I have to say, though, that she was very good about it. For starters, it didn't seem to come as any great shock to her. She seemed to have guessed as much and to be reasonably accepting. That is part of the paradox of my mother's nature – she will flat out PANIC over the tiniest most inconsequential thing, but tell her you've gone mad from hallucinogenics and she's just weirdly calm about it. Though I suppose it wasn't like I needed any further berating. I was recovering from some kind of episode, my life was stalled, I was living in my parent's house while my friends were travelling the world and making plans for their lives. Drugs are bad, I got the message. No lecture required.

To this day, I've no idea how much of my recovery I owe to the medication and how much simply to time and therapy. I'm sure it's a bit of a mix, but during those months at Fenvil I actually did start to feel better, little by little. I felt a bit stronger. I developed a new strategy regarding the obsessive thoughts whereby I started to detach from them somewhat. I started to realise that these thought spirals were fed by me and my panic and that I actually could decide not to engage with them. Of course this is not the case for everybody. I can only speak from my own experience and it's not as simple as deciding to get better and you will. I do feel that a huge factor in my recovery was luck. My parents had good jobs, I wasn't relying on the public health care system. I got a referral and was in a private hospital within days. I could afford to stop working and drop out of life. I had a family home to move back to when I couldn't take care of myself and was suicidal. I was supported in every way imaginable and I cannot overstate how much I think this contributed to my recovery.

For me, the process of getting better was baby steps forward and baby steps back and baby steps forward, and so on and so on. I stayed on Lexapro (the anti-depressant) for another two years. I didn't drink alcohol again for another four years; I never did drugs again! I began to recognise the cycle of relapse. Over the last 10 years, I have felt bad in my brain now and again but each episode seemed fainter and the time between each one got gradually longer and longer. And they never felt as powerful as those first months. When you know you can get through it once, you know you can get through it again.

BANANA BREAD

Moving back in with my parents may have seemed like a step back in terms of independence but actually living with them requires considerably more engagement in terms of 'what's for dinner?' They always seemed to me to eat like scavenging teenagers. The fridge is bare, devoid of anything more practical than a few jars of fuzzy chutney and a sad old hunk of cheese. Very unfortunate to weather a possible psychotic episode only to contract scurvy from moving back in with one's parents. I had been relying heavily on Himself to keep me fed and watered while navigating the dark, howling void of my illness, so when he left to go travelling and I moved back home, I needed to engage more with the simple act of nourishing myself. I was not a cook at this stage but I did love eating, so I had a pretty good sense of how to put a meal together. This banana bread toasted was a lovely, comforting supper. The eating I did then was just like the kind of living I was doing. Nothing too taxing or strenuous. Like my days, I kept my meals simple and not too complicated. It's a strange thing making your way through an illness, particularly one of the brain – it's all baby steps and softly softly. It's like a form of rehabilitation, but instead of regaining physical strength, you're slowly building mental resilience. **Serves 6–8**

- *125g butter*
- *1 teaspoon vanilla extract*
- *165g sugar*
- *235g self-raising flour*
- *1 teaspoon bicarbonate of soda*
- *1 teaspoon ground cinnamon*
- *2 eggs*
- *3 bananas, mashed*

Preheat the oven to 160°C/Gas 3. Line a loaf tin with baking paper. Place the butter, vanilla extract and sugar in the bowl of an electric mixer and cream together until light and fluffy. Sift the flour, bicarbonate of soda and cinnamon into a bowl.

Add 1 egg to the butter and sugar mixture and beat until it is thoroughly incorporated; repeat with the remaining egg. Scrape down the sides of the bowl with a spatula to ensure everything is fully mixed in.

With the mixer still running slowly, add half the mashed banana and half the sifted flour mixture, combine fully, then add the remaining mashed banana and the sifted flour mixture and mix to combine.

Pour the batter into the prepared tin and bake in the middle of the preheated oven for 1 hour–1 hour 10 minutes, or until golden and a skewer inserted into the centre of the loaf comes out clean.

FIG AND LEMON MARMALADE

I learned to make this jam in the first kitchen I worked in in New Zealand. It's pretty epic smeared along with some butter (never forget the butter) on the toasted banana bread. It makes a good gift, too, as people tend to be quite impressed with efforts in the field of marmalade. My advice is: never tell anyone how easy this is. **Makes 2 jars**

- *300g lemons, halved, pips removed and very thinly sliced*
- *250g dried figs, destemmed and quartered*
- *900ml water*
- *900g caster sugar*

Place the lemon slices in a large bowl. Add the fig quarters. Cover with the water and leave to stand overnight.

Place the fruit and water in a large, heavy-based saucepan and bring to the boil. Remove from the heat, add the sugar and stir to dissolve. Return to the heat and boil for approximately 40 minutes. There are two ways to know if this jam is done: Either boil it with a sugar thermometer and remove it from the heat when it reaches 105°C, or else, as it is thickening, spoon small amounts of jam onto a cold plate and chill in the fridge for a couple of minutes. This will give you an idea of what consistency the jam will be when cooled and will tell you when to take it off the heat.

After the jam has cooled store it in sterilised jars. If the cooled jam is too firm, loosen it up by stirring in a little boiled water.

BEANS ON TOAST

Being former cooks, myself and Himself lived for many years on a diet of cereal and beans on toast. That's the thing about cooking for a living, you really can't be bothered when it comes to feeding yourself. At some stage between getting married, getting a mortgage and getting a baby it seemed time to grow up. This *home-made*, not out-of-a-can beans on toast feels pretty grown up to me, what with the pancetta and Parmesan. It is also much tastier than the canned variety for not too much more effort. **Serves 3**

- *1 tablespoon olive oil*
- *1 onion, finely diced*
- *65g pancetta*
- *1 garlic clove, crushed*
- *1 bay leaf*
- *1 teaspoon paprika*
- *¼ teaspoon cayenne pepper*
- *2 teaspoons mustard powder*
- *65g tomato purée*
- *2 tablespoons Worcestershire sauce*
- *2 tablespoons golden syrup or brown sugar*
- *1½ teaspoons salt*
- *400ml water*
- *800g tinned butter or cannellini beans, drained*
- *toast, buttered spinach and Parmesan cheese shavings, to serve*

Heat the oil in a large saucepan over a medium heat. Add the onion and pancetta and sauté for about 5 minutes until soft and golden. Add the garlic, bay leaf, paprika, cayenne pepper and mustard powder. Stir thoroughly and cook for about 2 minutes, then add the tomato purée, Worcestershire sauce, golden syrup, salt and water.

Stir well, then increase the heat and bring the sauce to the boil. Reduce the heat and simmer for about 10 minutes, stirring frequently to prevent sticking. Add the beans and simmer for a further 10 minutes, until the liquid is thick and saucy and the beans are tender. Sometimes the beans can take in quite a bit of the liquid, so if it is drying out a bit, just add a little more water to loosen it up.

Serve on toast with buttered spinach and a generous sprinkling of Parmesan cheese shavings.

BAKED SAUSAGES WITH PEARS AND BLUE CHEESE

Nothing says home like bangers and mash, and this version has some nice seasonal twists. **Serves 2**

- 1 butternut squash, halved, peeled, deseeded and cut into chunks
- 1 tablespoon rapeseed oil
- 60g blue cheese
- 2 slices white bread
- 1 tablespoon butter
- 6 sausages
- 2 pears, thinly sliced
- 1 red onion, thinly sliced
- 1 tablespoon soft brown sugar
- 100ml white wine
- 2 tablespoons butter
- good pinch of ground nutmeg
- salt and freshly ground black pepper

Preheat the oven to 200°C/Gas 6. Toss the squash with the oil, then place in an ovenproof dish and roast in the preheated oven for 30–40 minutes until tender.

Meanwhile, blitz the cheese and bread together in a food processor. Melt the butter in an ovenproof frying pan over a medium heat, then add the sausages and brown all over.

Add the pears and onion to the pan and cook for about 5 minutes to soften, then sprinkle in the sugar and add the wine. Bring to the boil and simmer for 5 minutes to reduce the liquid.

Crumble the cheese and bread mix over the top of the mixture in the pan and bake in the oven for 5–10 minutes until the crumble topping is golden. Mash the squash with the butter, nutmeg and salt and pepper to taste, then top it with the sausage and pear bake to serve.

CHAPTER 11

K¡tchen*b!tch

In which I flee to New Zealand and somehow wind up WORKING AS A COOK, and find, to my amazement, that I love it.

I ACCIDENTALLY BECAME A COOK WHEN I ACCIDENTALLY ENDED UP LIVING IN New Zealand for two years. Being the proud owner of a degree in fine art, I found that I was qualified for virtually nothing. Up to that point I had worked in extremely undemanding roles. That was my MO – the less to do the better. When I was 16, I had worked as officially the world's slowest, worst cleaner in Barnacles Budget Accommodation in Temple Bar – a favourite among stag and hen parties and where I once picked up a bin full of sick. The bin was made of wicker and just sort of strained the sick all over my shoes. My main job was to get the stags and hens up in the morning for their 10.00 checkout, so I was pretty universally hated, like the woman who put the cat in the bin circa 2010 (remember her?), or Hitler.

The next job was in a restaurant in Dublin where I was the cliché clumsy waitress type. I spent my shifts there essentially flinging food and drink all over the customers. The last straw was an incident involving a diner and the tray I was carrying. I didn't hit him with it, that would actually have been slightly more forgivable. What I did instead was spend about five minutes pressing the tray into his forehead as I tried to get the order straight. I had my notepad on the tray and was effectively bracing the tray against his head. I even remember vaguely thinking that it was a much steadier surface to write on then usual, but I did not stop to investigate why. When the man's co-diners noticed what I was doing there was a bit of a kerfuffle, to which I did not respond well. I immediately went on the offensive and attacked the tray-bracer for being 'weird', and saying how 'utterly bizarre' it was for him to just sit there and let me press a tray against his head without saying a word.

My next job was in Paris where I worked for a brief stint as an artist's model. I was required to take my clothes off and keep still. You'd think that this would pose no problems and yet I still managed to cause some tension. I did not sit for large groups of students, you see, I worked for just one painter, so our sessions, to my mind, were quite intense one-to-one situations. I found the silence so bizarre. We were two people just sitting in a room doing nothing, one of whom was naked. I think I just forgot that he, of course, was not doing nothing, he was trying to work. I felt oddly compelled to make small talk, with which Robert would most grudgingly engage. I'd say he averaged one answer for every five questions I asked. I was trying to practise my shit French and I noticed that the one topic he did seem to take some interest in was the Troubles. My understanding of the Troubles would be hazy at best in English – in French I didn't have a hope. I think I managed to make some blunder regarding France's relationship with Belgium (another topic about which I know nothing), comparing that to the strained tensions between Ireland and England at the height of the Troubles. I realise now that France and Belgium are in fact great pals and that I should never talk about these things.

During my last two years at college I persisted in waitressing part time, and I also worked taking bets at the dogs. This was one of my favourite jobs of all time. Now, I'm not saying that trashy people go to the dogs, it's more like people just become that bit more trashy when at the dogs. It's like a person's inner Del Boy just comes out automatically when faced with greyhounds, leather-like carvery dinners, angry betters and mini pens. Further evidence of this came when a friend of mine who worked with me decided one night to make off with his cash bag. This was foolhardy. He made it as far as the gents before having an attack of anxiety and barricading himself in a stall.

The cash bags contained around 300 quid and about 30 or so people worked the tote each night. At the end of the night we balanced our own cash and returned the bags to the office. The tote paid our wages into our bank accounts. It really wouldn't be rocket science to track down the genius who fecked off with the cash bag. And for 300 quid, no less. He had to be coaxed out of the toilet, shaking like the soldier who always cracks up in war movies.

The all-time best thing about the tote was that they were so disorganised that hardly anyone in management seemed capable of enforcing a roster, so showing up or not showing up seemed to be largely at the employees' discretion. I did not have the discipline for this kind of set-up. I really need someone to be constantly berating me at all times to get any bit of work out of me.

I'm the person that finds myself exhausted just reading the attributes listed in job descriptions. This is before any work has even taken place yet. You know the sort of thing: Are you a self-starter, target-motivated, go-getter? I'm shattered just reading that. My next job, in the bookshop, was probably the first bit of self-motivating I'd ever had to do and we all saw how that worked out. Two months in and I threw in the towel and went full-tilt into a nervous breakdown.

With my varied and somewhat chequered work past it probably did not seem like I would make a very good chef. Cheffing requires stamina and the ability to take untold amounts of crap from your head chef, your manager, the customers, the suppliers – just everyone really. Everyone's giving you shedloads of shit while all you really want to do is go for a lie down in the dry goods store. I blagged my way into a job in a very busy café/restaurant in Queenstown on New Zealand's South Island by telling the head chef that while I had no training I had 'on-the-job experience'. That translated as back in Dublin when, as a waitress, I used to squirt coulis in a circle around a plate, blob a pre-made plastic-wrapped chocolate mousse on top and still forget, every single time, to remove the plastic wrapping first so as not to destroy the coulis circle.

Presumably if he didn't know I was lying from the off, he figured it out within the next hour when I dropped a commercial-sized container of mayonnaise onto a birthday cake that was to be collected for someone called Chanelle, and then proceeded to take half an hour to chop three onions before slicing my hand open with the knife and bleeding absolutely everywhere. Bodily fluids and kitchens really don't go and I assumed that I would never see the inside of a kitchen again. Incredibly, I got the job. On reflection, I realised that actually getting the job was even worse, as now I was that girl who'd fucked up Chanelle's birthday cake and then bled everywhere. And, yes, I was called the Bleeder for many months afterwards.

When you start on such a low in a new career it is almost liberating. The only way, after all, was up, unless I full-on killed someone with bad storage practices or something. Starting work in that kind of environment is pretty daunting, especially when you have no idea what you are doing, but from day one I knew cooking was something that I wanted to be good at. I was never shy about asking for help and I was lucky in that the chefs I worked with, despite very clearly regarding me as a complete joke of a person, were incredibly generous with their knowledge and time and patience and ciggies.

At the time it probably seemed like quite a random decision for someone who was still recovering from the trauma of mental illness to throw themselves into a stressful environment like a busy kitchen, but now it kind of makes sense to me. That first brush with your own vulnerability, whether it's an accident, physical illness, mental illness or just having a general life setback, can seriously knock you. You have to learn how to be yourself again. And I didn't really know who I was supposed to be. I was just making it up as I went along, but I think setting myself a target and getting to it went a huge way towards feeling stronger again.

My target was to get from kitchen low-life to being in charge of the pass. In a kitchen that size this is obviously not an emotional journey of epic proportions, but not completely easy either. For anyone who's never worked in a professional kitchen, here's a basic run down, drawn from my admittedly limited experience (I worked as a cook for about eight years, which is in fact only eight weeks in chef years). Dishies or KPs (kitchen porters) do the dishes and grunt prepping like washing bin liners full of spinach or juicing four crates of oranges a day. They are also the most chill component of your average kitchen team. If you need a tray back immediately expect to wash it yourself. Next up are the commis, who I generally think of as the kitchen bitches. They are usually pretty ambitious – after all no one gets into cooking to make salads and soups all day. Commis are eager little bastards. Sous chef and head chef are the big bastards who run the show with the iron fist and occasional unexpected tenderness of a hyena mother.

In a professional kitchen there is never an empty moment. You are either doing the ballet of service or the panicked prepping of a mofo. If you are neither doing service nor prepping, then you are cleaning. Breaks are fairly unheard of. Food is consumed in a grotesque squatting position over a bin. Minor injuries must be dealt with without breaking the flow of service. There will be no crying or a bathroom break until Table 6 have had their mains.

During service every chef has a station – you are solely responsible for organising your own station and ensuring you have all the necessary *mise en place* prepped and ready to go for the menu. A menu is broken down into components so that perhaps three people are cooking different aspects of one dish in a beautifully choreographed dance of stress, precision and heat to ensure that each element arrives to the chef on the pass at exactly the right time to be plated up, along with the other three dishes from that table's order. 'And the starters for Tables 2, 7 and 8.' 'And where's my soup for Table 9?' 'How long for 6's order?' Whoever is on the pass barks these questions all night long and generally runs the team like an army commando for the duration of service. They are looking at 20 checks, all with different stipulations and permutations and combinations of the menu. They call out the orders and direct the whole show, stacking dishes in an unending queue of catalogued urgency that feels like it will stretch on for ever when you're in it. On your station you receive your cue from the pass, immediately mentally slot the orders that are coming down the line into a constant flow of searing fish, deglazing pans, putting eggs in to poach, realising that you're a duck breast short, oh crap, crap, crap and timing, timing, timing. It's really fucking fun, if you like that sort of thing.

Obviously every kitchen is different and a lot of a kitchen's atmosphere comes from whoever is on the pass. To my mind screamers are the least frightening. They just want you to scream back at them, 'Yes, Chef!' Communication and shouting is of utmost importance. You can't just slip quietly behind someone in a kitchen or they'll accidently burn you or slash you. You must shout, panto-style, 'behind you', or 'on your left', or 'on your right' or, worst of all, when ducking under someone's bench to grab a pot, 'below you', which does unfortunately sound exactly like 'blow you'.

I gather that trends in kitchens these days are moving away from the shouty cliché (thank you, Ramsay), and kitchen life is becoming less of a hazing and a bit more joyful, which sounds much more appealing. Still, though, the argy-bargy is messy and fun. People often used to ask me if I didn't find that kind of work too stressful, but I don't think you would get into it if the mayhem and the pace didn't invigorate you. Also, the kitchen camaraderie is undeniable. In a good team you find you become like a dysfunctional family of sorts. You bitch about each other and at each other, then you cover for each other. It's close, at times a little too close.

Back in the restaurant in Queenstown over the course of a year I had worked my way up to the grill and then the pass, and I was loving it. At the time we had a particularly rowdy crew in the kitchen sharing the sous chef duties. The sous chef on shift worked a fairly gruelling 12–14-hour shift that started with baking for the day at 5.00 in the morning and wrapped up, if you were lucky, around the time dinner service was winding down. Most nights the crew would be in the pub, and whoever was on 'muffins' (as we called the early shift due to the baking aspect) would start a petition around 4.00 am or so to swap shifts.

The muffin shift was always a chaotic one. Whoever was doing it arrived at the restaurant at 5.00 am and spent the next two hours prepping 56 sweet muffins, 56 savoury muffins, 2 litres of hollandaise sauce, 3 litres of pancake batter, 6 litres of soup (the soup blender looked like a mini pneumatic drill) and a million other tiny jobs before the restaurant opened for breakfast and the dishy and the second chef started. It was a lot to get done and any disorganisation in the prep would invariably lead to a NIGHTMARE breakfast service, which has a knock-on effect on the whole day. Being late was out of the question. Hungover or still drunk was doable, but not late.

On one occasion a colleague, Ian, actually broke into my house through my bedroom window at just after 5.00 one morning to get my set of keys as he had lost his and was supposed to be opening up. This seemed like a totally reasonable thing to do. The clock was ticking and those muffins wouldn't bake themselves. Also, I have learned that a funny quirk of hollandaise sauce is that it immediately splits at the slightest inkling of stress. It's contrary that way and, sadly, usually irretrievable. Sometimes vigorously whisking in a teaspoon of warm water might, just might, save your ass.

As I said, hungover or drunk in that tumultuous kitchen was doable. However, tripping on hallucinogenic drugs was far more challenging. Don't worry, it's not me this time. In a dubious move, boy genius Ian (Ian again) had taken acid some hours before starting his shift. When he first arrived I noticed nothing amiss. However, when an order for pancakes came in, he proceeded to pour out three ladles of hollandaise sauce instead of batter onto the flat grill. The effect was pretty spectacular. Upon making contact with the hot surface the sauce immediately split, sending tiny beads of hot butter in every direction on the surface of the grill. I could see Ian, dumbfounded, was genuinely wondering whether this was really happening or whether it was a product of his hallucination. He was quickly dispatched to cold prep where he spent the rest of the day assembling sandwiches in an excruciatingly slow and painstaking fashion.

When I think back on my years in kitchens the thing that really dominated my experience was making hollandaise sauce, poaching eggs, cooking meat to fucking perfection (Take it off earlier than you think you should. Always.), learning how to get six uses out of one thing that's already prepped and losing all sensation in my fingers. And I loved it.

POACHED EGGS WITH CRUSHED WHITE BEANS

We all have a talent in this life. I always wanted to be one of those people who could pull out a guitar at a party or do cartwheels. Anything really would be better than the talent that I possess. You see, the great tragedy of my life is that my talent is so niche and obscure that it is rarely called for. I am an incredibly good egg poacher.

I wasn't born with this talent, I worked hard for it and paid in sweat – if that doesn't sound too disgusting. For virtually my whole 20s I worked as a cook, but professional egg poacher would really have been a more apt title. Everywhere I worked I would at some point display my egg-poaching talents and then be relegated to egg-poaching duties for the duration of my tenure there. Thus my greatest talent became my greatest downfall, since it stalled any hope of career advancement. Well, that's my theory, anyway, and I'm sticking to it.

One of the places I worked had an open kitchen with seating overlooking the stove area. All through my shift I had to poach eggs – among other things obviously – with an audience of curious onlookers. I noticed a lot of people seem to be truly fascinated with the process of poaching eggs. Among those who are ignorant of the method there seems to be a sense that egg-poaching is some kind of dark art. The Gift is practically a mark of evil, like speaking in tongues or having cloven hoofs.

After a while the onlookers started to request pointers and demonstrations. People seem to think there is a lot more to poaching eggs than there actually is. I started to throw in incongruous instructions, like close one eye when dropping the eggs into the pan, to see if anyone noticed. So what is the ultimate method for perfect poached eggs? Here goes: Bring a medium-sized saucepan of water to the boil with 1 tablespoon of white wine vinegar. Reduce the heat slightly, allowing the bubbles to settle somewhat. Using a spoon, spin the water (clockwise for me – I'm a bit anal) and drop the eggs in low to the surface. I crack them one-handed because I'm a bit of a show-boater like that. Some people recommend cracking the eggs into little ramekins first but that, my friends, is for pussies. **Serves 2**

- 200g tinned butter beans, drained
  and rinsed
- juice of ½ lemon
- 1 large garlic clove, peeled and
  crushed
- 1 tablespoon tahini
- 4 tablespoons olive oil, plus extra
  for brushing and drizzling
- ½ teaspoon salt
- 4 slices good white bread
- 100g halloumi cheese, cut into
  6-mm slices
- 2 pinches of sumac
- 4 eggs
- 1 tablespoon white wine vinegar
- buttered spinach or kale, to serve

Mash together the beans, lemon juice, garlic, tahini, oil and salt with a fork and set aside. Heat a griddle pan over a high heat, brush with a little of the remaining oil, add the cheese and fry for a few minutes on either side until crisp and golden, then set aside.

Meanwhile, fill a medium-sized saucepan with water, add the vinegar and bring to the boil. Reduce the heat slightly, swirl the water with a slotted spoon, then drop in the eggs low to the surface. Cook for 3–4 minutes, or to your liking, then remove from the water with a slotted spoon.

Brush the bread with a little oil and griddle in the pan until lightly charred and crispy. Arrange the toast on two plates, spread the mashed beans on the bread, top with the cheese, a good sprinkling of sumac, a drizzle of oil and the poached eggs. Serve with spinach or kale for a little green.

PISTACHIO-CRUSTED SALMON WITH HOLLANDAISE SAUCE

This is a fish special that I was very fond of putting on the menu in Vudu, my second restaurant job. The KP hated me for it as it was usually up to him to do the shelling of the pistachios. **Serves 4**

- 1 tablespoon cumin seeds
- 50g pistachio nuts (shelled weight)
- 10g flat-leaf parsley, roughly chopped
- zest of 1 lemon
- 2 garlic cloves, crushed
- 80g fresh breadcrumbs
- 1 tablespoon olive oil
- 4 salmon fillets, skin removed
- 2 teaspoons Dijon mustard
- new potatoes and buttered spinach, to serve

Hollandaise sauce
- 3 egg yolks
- 1 tablespoon white wine vinegar
- 200g butter, melted
- Tabasco sauce (optional)
- salt and pepper
-

Preheat the oven to 200°C/Gas 6. Line a baking tray with baking paper. Place a non-stick frying pan over a high heat and toast the cumin seeds for a couple of minutes to release the flavour. Place the cumin seeds, pistachio nuts, parsley and lemon zest in a food processor, along with the garlic and the breadcrumbs. Blitz the mixture for a couple of seconds to crush the nuts and combine all the ingredients, but leave it quite coarse.

Rub the oil into the mixture. Arrange the fillets on the prepared tray and smear each with a little mustard. Lightly press the breadcrumb mixture onto each fillet and bake in the preheated oven for 12–15 minutes, depending on how you like your salmon cooked. Serve with new potatoes and buttered spinach.

To make the hollandaise sauce, place the egg yolks in a metallic bowl and add the vinegar. Hold the bowl over a low–medium heat and whisk vigorously. Keep the eggs moving constantly – you want them to heat gently but never to scramble. If they are heating too fast

pull the bowl away from the heat and keep them moving. The eggs are thick enough when you can finish drawing a figure of eight on the surface before the '8' disappears.

Place the eggs on the counter carefully (the bowl may be hot), then add the melted butter in a thin stream, slowly at first, whisking constantly to incorporate. Once all the butter has been added the sauce should be thick and glossy. Check the seasoning, adding a little salt and pepper or Tabasco (if you're me!), and a splash of water if it needs to be thinned slightly.

RED ONION MARMALADE

This recipe will give you one jar of onion marmalade which can be called into service for any amount of fancifying of meals. Serve it on a cheese board, alongside a steak or even add some stock to make a sticky gravy for some juicy fat sausages. Seriously useful stuff, this, and just the kind of thing that is trotted out in many guises in the daily kitchen specials of a practical operation. **Makes 1 jar**

- 20g butter
- ½ teaspoon rapeseed oil
- 250g red onions, halved and sliced into half moons
- 1 garlic clove, sliced
- 20g sugar
- 1 teaspoon fresh thyme leaves
- 2 tablespoons balsamic vinegar
- 100ml red wine

Heat the butter and the oil in a large saucepan over a medium heat. Add the onions and garlic and cook gently until the onions are translucent.

Stir in the sugar and thyme, pour in the vinegar and wine, bring to the boil, then reduce the heat and simmer for about 15 minutes until the jam has thickened.

Remove from the heat, leave to cool and store in a sterilised jar in the fridge.

STEAK AND CHIPS WITH BÉARNAISE SAUCE

There is so much agonising over these three simple bits of nosh that I was tempted to not even include them in anticipation of the sheer arguing that would kick off in my own kitchen, never mind among the general population of readers. When you've got the likes of Escoffier, Ducasse and Harold McGee all unable to agree on something as basic as whether or not it is advisable to season a steak before, during or after cooking, then what hope do I have of offering up the definitive guide! What I offer instead is what I hope is a straightforward, tasty guide to the imperfect steak dinner. **Serves 2 (if you're still speaking after a 'to parboil or not to parboil chips' debate)**

- *2 generous handfuls of new potatoes, scrubbed and cut into chunks*
- *4 tablespoons olive oil*
- *1 fresh rosemary sprig, finely chopped*
- *handful of fresh tarragon, finely chopped*
- *1 portion of hollandaise sauce (see page 193)*
- *2 sirloin steaks, about 2.5cm thick, at room temperature*
- *1 tablespoon olive oil*
- *knob of butter*
- *sea salt flakes and freshly ground black pepper*

Preheat the oven to 200°C/Gas 6. Coat the potatoes with 3 tablespoons of the oil, scatter over the rosemary and season with salt and pepper. Bake in the preheated oven for 30–40 minutes until crisp, tossing a couple of times during the cooking process.

Make a cheat's béarnaise sauce by stirring the tarragon into the hollandaise sauce. Coat the steaks with the remaining oil and a little salt (I wait until they're in the pan before grinding the pepper over them so as not to burn the pepper).

Heat a non-stick frying pan over a high heat. Slap the steaks into the pan and cook for about 3 minutes on each side for rare (please don't eat your steak well done – in a kitchen if the chef is asked for steak well done he'll say something like 'kill it for the idiots on Table 9'). Add the butter to the pan when turning the steaks to keep them nice and moist. Transfer the steaks to a warmed plate and leave to rest for a few minutes before serving (the meat will continue to cook during resting).

* A good test for doneness is the cheek, chin, forehead test. Basically poke your steak as it's cooking – for rare it should feel soft like your cheek, for medium it is soft with a little bit of firmness like your chin, and for well done it's hard like your forehead and you've officially killed it. Congratulations, a cow has died in vain.

LAMB HOTPOT

In a professional kitchen a dish like this rich, hearty hotpot is an easy order that will give you a break in the middle of a full-tilt crazy dinner rush. There's always the pain-in-the-ass dishes on the menu that require about four pans on the hob at once AND a rake of irritating garnishes, so when you get an order for the total no-brainer dish it's always a welcome relief.

This is also a perfect meal for big family get-togethers. I'm a great believer in farming out the work of a dinner party to the guests. If you're ever coming to my house I'm likely to charge you with bringing something. I find the best policy in this instance is to be very specific and tell the person what to do so that you don't wind up with baked nachos accompanying the Thai curry.

This stew also works well with lamb shanks but Himself demanded that I make it with shoulder instead, as I was becoming all too fond of a little-known dance of my own devising – I like to call it the Harlem Shanks – and I was trotting it out every time I cooked this. The leftovers freeze well. **Serves 10 (generously)**

- *4 large tablespoons rapeseed oil per batch of lamb*
- *2kg lamb shoulder, trimmed and cubed*
- *6 onions, diced*
- *600g soft prunes*
- *4 teaspoons juniper berries, crushed*
- *1.5 litres red wine*
- *juice and zest of 2 oranges*
- *large handful of parsley, chopped*
- *salt and freshly ground black pepper*
- *mashed potato and roast carrots, to serve*

Heat the oil in a large saucepan over a medium heat. Add the lamb cubes in batches, season with a little salt and pepper and cook until browned all over. Transfer the browned meat to a dish as you go. When all the meat has been browned, set it aside.

Add the onions to the pan and cook them in the remaining oil and lamb juices until they are softened.

Return the browned meat cubes to the pan, add the prunes, juniper berries, wine and orange juice and zest and give it all a good stir. Increase the heat and bring to the boil. Cover and

simmer for about 2 hours 30 minutes, stirring
occasionally to prevent sticking.

When it's ready the lamb should be tender and
the sauce thickened. The prunes should have
broken down.

Check the seasoning and stir the parsley
through just before serving. Serve with mashed
potato and roast carrots.

CHAPTER 12

It was a *teenage wedding* and the OLD FOLKS wished them well

In which I just about talk

myself out of the proposed jilting and am

REASONABLY HAPPY that I did

(most days).

OKAY, IT WASN'T QUITE A TEENAGE WEDDING BUT IT WASN'T SO FAR OFF. WE WERE 26 and 27 years old respectively and, as I said previously, our parents were quietly and politely bemused by our notion to get married. For any other couple it probably wouldn't have seemed so young, but the implication seemed to be that if we were in any way 'proper' – you know, people with jobs and a plan – it wouldn't have been so bad. Up until this point we had been living the lives of students on a year out, only it had spanned six years and three continents. Our most recent abode had been a Nissan Urvan, and prior to that a two-man tent smaller than a sock drawer.

We had also lived in an assortment of house shares along the way, and one of the most memorable was in New Zealand. It housed a constantly changing line-up of loners and oddballs, with a professional benefits scammer who lived in the basement with his teenage son (who I strongly suspected cooked meth down there). An uncomfortable scenario heralded the end of our stay there when the meth son stole the car of one of the guys living upstairs and took it for a joyride through a nearby campsite. No one was injured, but as the car was stolen and the joyride took place at 9.30 at night the boy was in breach of his curfew, one of the conditions of his release from a juvenile detention centre, and the case actually went to trial of sorts. Way more awkward than flatmate fights about eating the last of the cereal.

After the joyriding slash suspected meth cooking we decided to get a lease of our own so that we could better vet our potential flatmates. We managed to secure a large rambling house on a hill above Queenstown overlooking the vast Lake Wakatipu. We had the crumbling basement quarters, which doubled as rehearsal space for Himself's band at the time, Magnum Force. Four bedrooms upstairs housed whomsoever should make the cut during our rigorous housemate screening system.

Himself and I, being the leaseholders, had the job of interviewing potential flatmates. Usually we operated a democracy in the house around who should move in and tried to ensure that current housemates met prospective housemates. On one occasion, however, I offered the room to a guy called Ed without running him past the others. On the day he was supposed to be moving in there was no sign of his arrival except for a bag of clothes that appeared to have been stuffed through the window into the room.

That night the housemates were relaxing in the communal living space when a commotion was heard on the front lawn. All six of us came out front to find Ed, slumped, supported by two friends, being dragged up the driveway. Ed was clearly off his head and I could practically hear everyone thinking, 'Who the fuck is this guy and why is he moving in with us?'

'Where's he sleeping?' asked one of Ed's friends. I pointed inside the house. 'First on the right.' The housemates moved as one to watch Ed's progress down the hall. Suddenly Ed roared to life for a moment. 'Got to piss,' he said, attempting to open his pants. 'No!' everyone shouted in unison. The friends immediately changed course and now eight people were trying to bundle Ed into the main bathroom. We just about got him in there but not quite to the toilet, unfortunately. He'd somehow got his willy in hand and proceeded to piss all over the bathroom, dousing the six toothbrushes by the sink and two of his new housemates in the process.

The next day Ed made an enormous breakfast for his new roomies to apologise for weeing on everyone. Thankfully, he became a favourite among the flatmates. He was a bit of a force of nature. He was a chef, naturally, and was always going on or coming off a bender, or punching his boss, or baking I'm sorry cakes for punching his boss. He was a mega downhill biker and appeared to be genuinely quite fearless. He had survived a crazy car accident in his teens, not that Ed would ever mention this. I think I learned this from his mother, who seemed as besotted and bemused by Ed as anyone else who ever met him. He was full of charisma and found everything hilarious. His party piece was snapping his dodgy shoulder back into place whenever it 'popped out'. It was disgusting.

One night the housemates were sitting around watching the TV when the resident cat, Dorji, jumped down off a high shelf, causing the room to shake. Dorji was as fat as any cat can be, so when the room shook we thought nothing of it for a moment. The house was mostly constructed out of plywood and masking tape, so a particularly violent sneeze could rattle the windows. After a few minutes it began to dawn on us that the shaking was not subsiding and that now the walls appeared to be swaying. 'I think it's an earthquake,' someone said.

No one knew what to do in an earthquake, so we immediately did the worst thing possible and ran outside. The sensation was crazy, the road beneath us was jerking back and forth while the telephone poles, trees and electrical lines swayed overhead. We realised that Ed wasn't with us, 'He's still inside, in the shower!' someone shouted, panicked. I ran back down to the house and shouted through Ed's window, but no sign of him. After a few more minutes, the quake calmed and we trooped back inside. The shower was still going and Ed ambled out in a towel a few minutes later. When we fell upon him asking if was he all right, he clammed up. 'Yeah, I'm fine, nothing's wrong,' he shot back defensively. 'But there was an earthquake, Ed,' I explained, confused.

'Ahhh, thank fuck, I was freaking out. I thought I was having an acid flashback in there.' He cheered up immediately and popped off to get dressed.

The house's line-up shifted around frequently but during a particularly harmonious time there three out of the five members of Magnum Force resided at 12 Thompson Street. They practised covers of The Ramones, The Kinks, The Darkness and Dexy's Midnight Runners in the basement, aka my bedroom. They played gigs around town and also in our living-room, where they had installed a wooden stage, smoke machine and an ambitious lighting set-up. I came home from work one night to a sandwich board erected outside my house proclaiming 'FREE GIG', and a flaming oil drum burning hobo-style on the front lawn. Unsurprisingly, the next day our letting agent made a surprise visit, presumably alerted by disgruntled neighbours. The front room was still showing signs of having recently been occupied by about 85 friends and randomers, while the upended sandwich board and scorched lawn provided further damning evidence that we were perhaps not respecting the rules of our lease. We were given 24 hours to dismantle the stage and cop on, which we duly did.

During this time the first rumblings of the world financial crisis were stirring. Himself and I were planning to blow all our savings in Southeast Asia on an extended trip, when he called me into the living-room to watch scenes on TV of Lehman Brothers employees leaving the building with their possessions in boxes after the historic bank filed for bankruptcy. 'I don't think we should go travelling right now,' he explained. I, being totally ignorant of financial matters, wanted to withdraw all our money immediately and buy krugerrands and tinned goods. His response was more measured. All our money was in Kiwi dollars. In amongst the earthquakes and joyriding and living-room stock we had been working multiple jobs to save for our trip. That money was apparently about as good as Monopoly money, I learned. I spoke to the Bitch Herd back in Dublin, some of whom had been out of work for more than a year. The outlook was pretty bleak. We needed to get back to Europe but were afraid we wouldn't have a hope of getting work.

Several of the chefs I worked with had done winter seasons in the French Alps and this started to look like a very appealing prospect. Cooking, snowboarding, eating, sleeping and partying in return for a room and all the cheese you can eat. We prepared to leave New Zealand after two years there. We threw a huge party, Magnum Force played a farewell gig, we said goodbye to friends and embarked on the epic journey home. The flight was 36 hours with a stop-over in Hong Kong. For budget reasons we took a nine-hour bus to the airport. It was long. The bus wasn't a great idea.

Home in autumn 2009 was a strange place. I was apprehensive about returning to the settings were I had felt so mad before. Also, just a few months earlier I had weaned myself off the Lexapro. Being away and coming back was a bit alienating. Every sentence seemed to start with 'While you were away … ', and anything I could think of to say began with 'In New Zealand … '. The Bitch Herd were still close but it was clear that individually we were moving in different directions. Fat Tits was doing her PhD, Jenga was doing a post-grad and back-to-back internships, while Jessom was in retail and had just ditched a guy whom we had all hated. Also, the last time we had spent significant time together I'd been really out of it. Now here I was, back, but still in some way different. I was guarded and careful with myself, afraid of letting the madness back in. I also felt guilty about what felt like ducking out and dodging what the country was going through. We said our goodbyes just a few weeks after the hellos and got on a plane to France, where we spent the next four years on and off. Snowboarding in the winter, cycling in the summer, living as cheaply as we could and never thinking too far ahead.

This is where, I gather, our parents got the idea that we were probably not mature enough to get married. A few months after Himself had proposed and I had finally calmed down enough to actually be able to talk about the wedding we drove our van down to northern Spain to spend a week with my parents and Himself's mother. We had been doing odd jobs for cash in our home in the Alps to save up for food and gas money. The cash was stashed in secret cubbies dotted around the van and one day in Spain, when my mother spotted me unearthing a crumpled 20 from a secret square cut out of the back of the driver's seat, I imagine I never seemed less like her daughter.

To be fair, they weren't disapproving so much as confused. We were just living in a very different world from theirs. My mother works in the media, and we lived with no electricity, reading to each other in the evening at bedtime, and checking in with email at most every couple of weeks. In the van, we ate canned goods and foraged for tiny Alpine raspberries and anaemic-looking wild rhubarb – it took pretty much an entire bush to make one crumble with those skinny stalks. While other folks had a blow-dry once a week and watched *The X Factor*, I showered with a two-litre bottle punched with holes and hung from a tree and had to get creative about going to the loo.

When you live off the grid like this for even a short time you just can't connect with things happening on social media. You can remain mercifully unaware of the *Daily Mail* for months at a time. You can remain unshowered for months at a time. It's liberating and I miss it. I knew most assuredly that my vagabond days were over once my bourgeois yearning for an extension and a new kitchen kicked in, though that was still a few years off.

During that week in Spain the arguments raged over the ins and outs of us getting married, but six months later we did it anyway. Right up to the morning of the wedding I was feeling fairly dubious. I sat in a taxi outside the registry office with Jenga and Jessom, while the rain hammered down outside, and we debated making a break for Holyhead. Eventually we went inside and I walked down the sort of aisle thingy and joined Himself at the desk. In an unusual move he'd opted for a kilt for his wedding attire (unusual in that he has absolutely no Scottish connection whatsoever). He looked well in it. As we took our seats, my eye strayed to his lap where, nestled in his crotch, was a small furry sporran (a type of Scottish man-purse). The sight of the furry purse managed to be both jarring and comforting to me at the exact same time. 'Okay,' I thought to myself, 'I still have absolutely no idea how this marriage thing is going to pan out, but if you're going to marry anybody it has to be this man.'

My seasoned advice as someone who has weathered four whole years of marriage is marry someone unconventional who understands you, and who will always be full of furry little surprises. And, yes, I know how that sounds, and I'm comfortable with that.

When planning a wedding for yourself that you are iffy about attending it is wise to keep the ceremony section of the thing pretty intimate. This will minimise embarrassment for the jilted party and give you a far better chance of forgiveness from said jilted party should you try to make a case for attending the wedding meal despite having skipped the actual marriage portion of the day. In the end, luckily, it didn't come to this and Himself and I did indeed sign that lovely document, which means he is contractually obliged to fancy me, make the tea and put out the bins for the rest of our lives.

Our wedding party that night was memorable for the people in attendance as it had a kind of Titanic-style, going-down-with-the-ship disaster vibe about it. Guests were corralled inside a large canvas tent while a full-scale storm raged outside. My poor choice of flooring (or lack thereof) inside the tent meant that most people were up to their ankles in flood water and just about managed to spit out 'Congratulations' from between gritted teeth, before scurrying off to try and reach higher ground somewhere between the bar and Table 3.

I think I was fairly universally hated at this thing. This became particularly clear when my mother gave a speech detailing my every transgression and stubborn disregarding of her views between the years 1987 to 2012. The speech also seemed to imply that I was in some way responsible for the terrible weather and that if I had just listened to her about doing an extra subject for the Leaving we wouldn't all be in this mess now, ruining our good shoes and drinking through our misery. This seemed like a bit of a stretch, but she is a persuasive and impassioned public speaker. The whole speech was fairly tough going for me, though everyone else thought it was a 'scream'. I can't wait for her eulogy, when it'll be payback time. As the night wore on and the water level continued to rise the whole party took on the bacchanalian abandon of a hooley down in steerage. The iceberg has hit, nothing to do now but kick off the shoes and go for a paddle on the dance floor. It was brilliant.

The food was a Lebanese-style feast cooked by the fantastic Kate Lyons who, as luck would have it, had a strong connection with that part of the world. Tables of 10 enjoyed a family-style sit-down meal of mezze plates, chargrilled lamb, falafel, stuffed vine leaves, fattoush, grilled halloumi and so much more. It was, to this day, one of my favourite meals. These recipes are the staples of our household and always remind me of that day and Himself's creepy little furry purse. It was definitely worth going through with it.

FLATBREADS

Crap pitta breads are a real bugbear of mine. You know the kind of anaemic-looking floppy things that more closely resemble a flap of foot skin than the delicious, crispy, oily, salty stuff of life. These bad boys are the ultimate vehicle for any blended garlic-loaded dip you care to mention and can be cooked in advance. **Makes 6–8**

- *200g plain flour, plus extra for dusting*
- *½ teaspoon salt*
- *½ teaspoon dried yeast*
- *130ml lukewarm water*
- *1 tablespoon olive oil, plus extra for oiling and brushing*
- *rapeseed oil, for cooking*
- *a few fresh rosemary sprigs*
- *sea salt flakes*

Mix the flour and ½ teaspoon of salt together in a bowl. Dissolve the yeast in the water and leave to stand for a few minutes until bubbles to rise to the surface.

Make a little well in the flour and pour in the yeast mixture and the olive oil. Using your hands, bring the dry and wet ingredients together to form a smooth dough. Knead the dough on a surface lightly dusted with flour for about 5 minutes.

Slick a clean bowl with a little olive oil and place the kneaded dough inside. Cover with a clean tea towel and leave to prove in a warm place for about 1 hour. Knock back the dough and place it on a work surface. Cut the dough into 8 small pieces, shape each piece into a ball and roll out thinly to the size of a pitta bread. Brush with olive oil and tuck the rosemary sprigs into the dough.

Heat a little rapeseed oil in a non-stick frying pan over a high heat. Cook the flatbreads one or two at a time for 1–2 minutes on each side. They will puff up slightly and become crisp. Wipe the pan clean between each batch and add a little more oil for the next two flatbreads.

If serving these at a dinner, cook them in advance and then crisp them up for about five minutes in a hot oven (200°C/Gas 6) just before serving.

FETA DIP

Serves 6

- 200g Greek-style yogurt
- 100g feta cheese
- 3 tablespoons olive oil
- juice of ½ lemon
- sea salt and freshly ground black pepper, to taste
- ½ teaspoon sumac, to serve (optional)

Place the yogurt, cheese, oil, lemon juice and salt and pepper in a food processor and pulse until combined. Alternatively, roughly mash them together with a fork.

Transfer to a serving bowl, sprinkle over the sumac, if using, and serve.

Flat breads, feta dip, baba ganoush, falafel and lamb tagine

BABA GHANOUSH AND HAZELNUT DUKKAH

Here is one of the aforementioned garlic-loaded dips. Anyone who has yet to make baba ghanoush is about to be wowed by the transformation a humble aubergine goes through when simply pricked and flung into the oven for a bit. It's one of the most impressive metamorphoses in the culinary world, akin to that of roasting garlic. Hmmmmm, roast garlic …

Back to the baba, it's fun to say, good to eat and easy to make. **Serves 6**

- 2 aubergines
- 2 garlic cloves, crushed
- 2 tablespoons tahini
- juice of ½ lemon
- 2 tablespoons olive oil
- salt

Hazelnut dukkah
- 100g hazelnuts
- 80g sesame seeds
- 2 tablespoons cumin seeds
- good olive oil, to serve

Preheat the oven to 200°C/Gas 6. Stab the whole aubergines all over with a fork and put them in the preheated oven for about 30 minutes until soft and squidgy. Set aside in a bowl, cover with clingfilm and leave to cool, then tear away the dark skins and place the soft flesh in the food processor along with the garlic, tahini, lemon juice, oil and a little salt. Blend until smooth.

To make the dukkah, place the hazelnuts on a baking tray and toast in the oven for about 3 minutes, keeping an eye on them, as nuts burn quickly. Rub them in a clean tea towel to remove as much of the skins as possible, then place in the food processor.

Toast the sesame seeds in a dry non-stick frying pan until golden and add to the hazelnuts. Wipe the pan clean and toast the cumin seeds for a couple of minutes until the aroma is released and the seeds begin to pop. Add these to the food processor and coarsely blend the dukkah together. Serve with the baba ghanoush.

FALAFEL

Before anyone jumps down my throat, I know that in an ideal world the chickpeas used in falafel should be of the dried variety, not tinned. However, in general, I am very far from being prepared and organised enough for that, so while purists may baulk, I say tinned work just as well. As a way of making up for this blasphemy I will, however, be deep-frying these little beauties, because that is the only way to truly enjoy a crispy on the outside juicy on the inside falafel. Also, I believe that when deep-fried correctly falafel don't take on as much oil as you might think. That is my theory and I'm clinging to it. **Makes 10**

- 400g tinned chickpeas, drained and rinsed
- 1 small red onion, finely diced
- 2 garlic cloves, crushed
- handful each of fresh mint, fresh parsley and fresh coriander, picked and chopped
- 1 teaspoon ground cumin
- 2 tablespoons plain flour
- 1 ½ teaspoons salt
- ½ teaspoon baking powder
- sunflower oil, for frying
- flatbreads (see page 212), salad and tahini dressing (see page 74) to serve

Mash the chickpeas in a bowl using a potato masher (doing this by hand prevents them turning into a paste), then add the add onion, garlic, herbs, cumin, flour, salt and baking powder. Shape the mixture into small, round patties and chill in the fridge for 30 minutes.

Heat sunflower oil to a depth of 5cm in a small saucepan over a medium heat. The oil is ready when a little bit of the mixture immediately sizzles and pops back to the surface when dropped in.

Fry the falafel in batches of four until golden brown. Drain on kitchen paper. Serve with flatbreads, salad and tahini dressing.

LAMB TAGINE

This is truly one of the tastiest meals I've ever had and so worth the extra bit of cooking time. **Serves 2, with a bit left over for lunch**

- 2 tablespoons sunflower oil, plus extra if needed
- 500g lamb shoulder, diced
- 1 onion, roughly chopped
- 2 garlic cloves, finely sliced
- 2 teaspoons ground coriander
- 2 teaspoons ground cumin
- 1 teaspoon turmeric
- 1 teaspoon ground cinnamon
- ½ teaspoon cayenne pepper
- 4 tablespoons ground almonds
- zest and juice of 1 orange
- 300ml chicken stock
- 15 dried dates, stoned and chopped
- salt and freshly ground black pepper
- couscous, toasted flaked almonds and roughly chopped fresh coriander, to serve

Heat the oil in a large saucepan, add the lamb in batches and cook until browned all over, then remove from the pan and set aside. In the same pan, sweat the onion and garlic. Stir in the ground coriander, cumin, turmeric, cinnamon and cayenne pepper. If the mixture looks dry, add a little more oil. Cook for about 5 minutes. Return the meat to the pan and stir well to coat.

Add the ground almonds and cook for a further 5 minutes. Add the orange zest and juice, stock and dates. Bring to the boil, then reduce to a simmer, cover and cook for about 1 hour, stirring frequently. Season to taste with salt and pepper.

Serve with couscous and garnish with a sprinkle of toasted almonds and chopped coriander.

CHAPTER 13

My *INSANE* love of granola (and how I didn't cop for three months that I was pregnant)

BAM!

In which I get the shock of my life

by getting pregnant.

SO, THERE I WAS, TUCKING INTO MY THIRD BOWL OF GRANOLA OF THE DAY WHEN I received The Text. It was the text we had all been waiting for. He had arrived: our brand-new nephew.

We were summoned to the hospital for some 'Ooohhing' and 'Aaahhhhing'. Himself collected me on his way. I hopped into the car, dribbling milk and oats down my front and prompting him to smirk, 'Another granola day?' 'Maybe,' I replied, a bit irked that he had caught me.

Of late, I had become enamoured of this extremely tasty, but very, very expensive granola. I had taken to stashing boxes around the house to try to conceal the sheer volume I had been consuming. In Himself's eyes, this was a luxury item – especially as a box cost €6.50 and contained roughly three bowls' worth of granola.

At the hospital, being the semi-newly wedded girl and, therefore, apparently gagging to be impregnated, the baby was thrust at me. I was terrified and profoundly intimidated by just how tiny he was. I kissed his head and then had a flash of where, until quite recently, his head had been. I signalled helplessly to Himself, who casually took the baby and rocked him like some kind of seasoned wet nurse. I should have been suspicious, but was actually just relieved to have been relieved of baby.

A few days later, at work, I was tasting a big batch of hollandaise sauce. It tasted awful, and I was on the verge of ditching the whole three litres (and anyone who's ever made three litres of hollandaise sauce knows just how heartbreaking starting from scratch was going to be) when my colleague tasted it and pronounced it delicious. Curiouser and curiouser.

I then spent the next two days in the worst mood of my life. I cried for no reason. I screamed at my friend in work for changing Table 2's order roughly eight seconds after giving it to me. Well, you all know where this one's going.

I reckon the actual location in which one conceives a baby is pretty telling as to how premeditated the act was. In the case of myself and Himself, I'm presuming (though I can't be sure) that the joyous union took place in our bed of that time – a bunk bed in my father-in-law's house. I think this is a fairly clear indication of how baby-ready we were. I had recently come off my long-term contraception and was using two other admittedly slightly more low-fi methods, the details of which I shall spare you. I had never had anything resembling a normal cycle since being on birth control for 10 years, and I wanted to lay off the hormones for a while and resume normal service in the ovaries department.

Nothing seemed amiss beyond the passionate reaction to Table 2's order change and feeling a bit tired. But then I worked standing for 10 hours a day, so feeling tired was reasonable. I was doing a bit of freelance writing on top of cooking and was transcribing an interview with an artist one night. As I sat there listening to her describing how she had realised that she was pregnant with her son, alarm bells started ringing. It was all sounding unnervingly familiar. Things tasting odd, wild emotions, cramps.

I went to the pharmacy immediately and was instructed by the woman at the till to wait until the morning for the most accurate results. Incredibly, I did sleep that night. Himself had brushed off my suspicions as nothing more than my usual paranoia about becoming pregnant – throughout my 20s he had witnessed frequent unfounded panics. I was the girl who cried 'baby'.

The next morning I went to the loo when the alarm went off at 6.00. I'd nearly forgotten about the test until I spotted it in the bathroom where I'd left it the night before to remind myself. I'd calmed down considerably at this stage and just did the test casually as it was there anyway. I watched the tide of wee pass through the little window on the test and nothing appeared. It remained blank. Relieved, I flushed the loo and started to brush my teeth. When I was finished I took one more quick glance at the test before popping it in the bin, only to discover that it was now reading positive.

For a few seconds the shock was so physical that my eyesight sort of blurred in and out of focus. It reminded me of those dolly zoom shots in *Vertigo* and *Jaws*, like a sensation of falling away from myself. I staggered back to the bedroom and lurched into the bed beside Himself. I never got to utter those unforgettable words, 'You're going to be a father.' Instead I just kind of lay there shaking until he groggily woke up and said, 'What's wrong?', and then, when I didn't respond, sat bolt upright and said, 'Jesus, did you just take that test?'

To say that we were woefully unprepared would be too generous. We were living in the dining-room of my father-in-law's house, saving for a mortgage, sleeping in a bunk bed and eating cereal for dinner every night. We had no plan. We had no insurance. There were no babies in our lives, we had no idea how to deal with babies. We were the babies.

Himself was quicker to the joy than I was. He got on board with the total wrong exit our life had just taken off the roundabout called 'ambling through our 20s' the very instant he saw that wee stick. His willingness to be in proximity to, and even touch the wee stick also seemed to confirm this. For me, I was 27 and scared. Which sounds completely lame, since I could've been 17 and scared, but there you have it, it can be a shock at any age.

First on the agenda was to find out just how pregnant I actually was. I presumed I'd go to the doctor who would cut me in half and count the rings. The reality was both easier and weirdly harder than that. She asked me when my last period was. I had no idea, given my elusive womanly cycle. 'November 2006?' I offered. At this, the doctor understandably looked dubious about my procreating qualifications. I was dispatched to Holles Street to determine the age of my foetus. It was nerve-wracking not knowing how long Yer Man had been in there and just what kind of mother I'd been to him so far in his young, barely started life.

It was strange to think that I'd been carrying around a secret little stowaway without realising it, mad that Himself (who I'd always assumed would have fairly lethargic sperm anyway) had slipped one of his guys past my defences. Yet there he was on the black screen at the hospital, a little kidney bean, already with arms and legs dancing and flailing about as if to say, 'Hi guys, it's me, I'm here!' I was about 11 weeks pregnant. There was no denying it. I cried a lot.

I cried at work in the dry store, among the sacks of flour and boxes of chocolate. My pal who made the coffees knew instantly. Everyone copped it immediately. Even the gang on Table 8 could tell I was doing battle with the raging onslaught of pregnancy hormones. Very early one morning our cheese delivery guy arrived to find me sitting outside the door trying to talk myself down from some intense morning sickness. I was still not visibly pregnant and made some mutterings about a heavy night. He looked suspicious. 'Aren't you your man from the Powerscourt café's girlfriend?' he said. Himself's kitchen was also one of his accounts. 'MMMMmm,' I moaned in the affirmative, as I lurched past him, deeply nauseated by the smell of his pungent products, and into the loo to puke my guts out. I washed my face and returned to apologise. He was smiling in a knowing way. 'That poor fella's in big trouble,' he said, smirking. 'What??? I was out last night,' I lied defensively. 'Ha!' he barked. 'In your condition? No way … ', and ambled on his way.

I was rumbled immediately by virtually everyone. My cousin said she could tell by my hips. Jenga knew because I ordered granola with a side of onion rings at breakfast. Jessom knew because I bought a larger size in jeans than I usually take from her shop. My father-in-law, with whom we lived at the time, figured it out because I went to bed around 7.00 every night for six weeks. My mother took one look at my nervous smile and said, 'You're pregnant', in the same tone you would use to say 'You're an idiot'. 'Well … yes,' I replied carefully. She tried to look happy about this but she's really crap at concealing her emotions. My mother-in-law said, 'What? Are babies having babies now?!' The only parent who seemed to respond to the news with any genuinely warm feelings was my dad, whose mental faculties, let's face it, were extremely compromised at this stage.

And I could totally understand their scepticism, because I was feeling the exact same way. I didn't know any babies, I wouldn't know what to be doing with a baby. I was, my mother always seemed to imply, barely holding my own life together, never mind being responsible for another's life. I wanted out. I thought about how it would feel to be standing on the rolling deck of a ferry to England.

A few days later I started to bleed when we were out for lunch with friends. I told Himself to go on to the pub with the others. I didn't want them to think that there was anything wrong. And maybe I wanted to be alone with my baby, to will him to stay. I got a taxi home, paralysed with panic in the back seat. Then I lay in bed and howled all afternoon. 'I want you, I need you, you're wanted, you're loved. Stay, stay, stay. Please stay.'

MAPLE AND CINNAMON GRANOLA

The expensive granola that sustained the baby for the first couple of months of gestation had to go when we realised that we would soon be buying nappies and iPhone 6s for our impending offspring. This is a nice classic granola that I particularly love with warm milk in winter. It also makes a good base recipe from which you can play around with your own permutations and combinations of nuts and dried fruit. **Serves 6**

- 100ml sunflower oil
- 100ml maple syrup
- 30g dark brown sugar
- 2 teaspoons ground cinnamon
- 500g jumbo oats
- 150g desiccated coconut
- 100g dried cranberries
- 100g toasted pecan nuts

Preheat the oven to 200°C/Gas 6. Line a roasting tin with baking paper. Put the oil, maple syrup and sugar into a saucepan over a medium heat. Stir well to combine and heat, stirring, until the sugar has melted.

Put the cinnamon, oats and coconut into a large bowl and mix well. Pour over the oil, sugar and maple syrup mixture and stir well to evenly coat the oats.

Pour the granola into the prepared tin and spread it out evenly. Toast the granola in the preheated oven for about 20–30 minutes, giving it a good stir every 5 minutes, until golden. Leave to cool completely, then add the cranberries and nuts. Store in an airtight jar or a Tupperware container.

BEER BREAD PIZZA

The main advantage of gestation was a constant supply of snacks conveyed to my mouth by the long-suffering Himself. He fast became used to my chronic eating jags. One week I was obsessed with hot dogs, the next Pop-Tarts. As culinary obsessions go these are not very highbrow, but at least they are convenient to cook, requiring virtually no effort on the part of Himself. One eating jag I took up was considerably more demanding: home-made anchovy pizza. And I wasn't taking no for an answer. I had four anchovy pizzas in one three-day period. The problem with home-made pizza is that it's a bit of a palaver, what with proving the dough and making the tomato sauce. This led to a bit of research on my part. The next night saw me lying on the couch barking instructions from underneath my considerable bump to a flour-covered Himself toiling in the little kitchen. This beer bread pizza dough gives a very thin, biscuity base which, while not as light as a traditional base, is still very tasty and wonderfully convenient, as there is absolutely no proving required. This is particularly pertinent when there is an angry little foetus rapping away on the inside of your tummy demanding anchovies. **Serves 4 as dinner (makes 2 pizzas)**

- 400g plain flour, plus extra for dusting
- 1 tablespoon baking powder
- 1 teaspoon salt
- 300ml beer
- 4 tablespoons harissa
- 8 tablespoon tomato purée
- 8 tablespoons passata

- 3 x 125g balls buffalo mozzarella cheese
- 2 tablespoons olive oil
- about 10 anchovy fillets
- sea salt and freshly ground black pepper
- pinch of dried mixed herbs

Preheat the oven to 230°C/Gas 8. Put two rectangular baking trays, at least 2cm deep, in the oven to heat.

Put the flour, baking powder and salt into a large bowl and mix together. Make a well in the centre of the mixture and pour in the beer, a little at a time, mixing everything together with your hand to make a soft dough. If the mixture is a little sticky, add a sprinkling of flour.

Turn out the dough onto a surface lightly dusted with flour and knead for about 3 minutes.

In a bowl, combine the harissa, tomato purée and passata. Tear the cheese into pieces. Divide the dough into two pieces and roll out each piece to a thickness of about 1 cm and a diameter of 25–30cm. Take the hot baking trays out of the oven and brush with oil. Place the pizza bases on the trays and flatten out the dough, using your hand if necessary.

Spread the harissa mixture evenly over the pizza bases, scatter over the anchovies and cover with the cheese. Season with salt and pepper.

Return the trays to the oven for 15–20 minutes, or until the cheese has melted and the bases have risen slightly and are golden around the edges and the undersides.

Leave to cool slightly in the trays, then slide out onto a large board to slice.

CARAMEL CRUMBLE SLICES

Being the heroic vessel generously propagating his seed, I was on the receiving end of a lot of Himself's culinary talents during this time. Usually he would ignore my pleas for cakes and treats (all things sweet being his specialty), pinching my chub and saying 'the last thing you need is a caramel crumble slice'. Now that the chub was warranted, however, he cheerfully plied me with all the confectionary delights he'd been withholding. When I was pregnant he worked as a pastry chef in a prominent four-star Dublin hotel, which was serendipitous, to say the least. **Makes 16**

- *110g butter, plus extra for greasing*
- *200g sugar*
- *270g plain flour*
- *50g cocoa powder*

Caramel
- *160g butter*
- *110g golden syrup*
- *395ml tinned condensed milk*

Preheat the oven to 150°C/Gas 2. Grease a 25-cm square cake tin and line with baking paper.

Put the butter and the sugar into the bowl of an electric mixer and cream together until pale and fluffy. Add the flour and cocoa powder, then beat gently until the mixture resembles coarse breadcrumbs. Do not over-mix.

Firmly press two-thirds of this mixture into the prepared tin and bake in the preheated oven for 20 minutes, then leave to cool in the tin. Do not switch off the oven.

Meanwhile, to make the caramel, put all the ingredients in a saucepan over a medium heat and stir until melted, combined and slightly thickened, then pour it over the base. Crumble the remaining base mixture over the top.

Bake for a further 15–20 minutes – the caramel will thicken further. Leave to stand for 4 hours, or overnight, or chill in the freezer for about 20 minutes. Cut into slices and serve.

CHAPTER 14

Food to eat while pregnant (and once more *teetering* on the verge of crazy)

In which I definitely don't take

being pregnant very well. Cue A LOT

OF CRYING and a gradual

return to crazy.

FOR THE FIRST FEW MONTHS OF BEING PREGNANT, I WOULD GO INTO THE bathroom to cry.

Himself would come to the door and ask 'Is it a sad wee?' It was a sad wee, but sad in a strangely unfocused way that was impossible to articulate, even to myself. When you are pregnant and you didn't really set out to be, it is a difficult position to be in. As the proud new owner of a foetus, you are not really allowed to be anything less than joyful and glowing. And let's not forget grateful. This is hard to take when the whole enterprise has been foisted on you, quite out of the blue, after some sketchy contraceptive methods and a bottle of Buckfast.

After the bleeding and pain during early pregnancy I'd had an inkling of just how conflicted I was feeling about the pregnancy. On the one hand I was petrified at the prospect of becoming a parent and on the other I was wild and terrified of losing the baby.

By around the sixth month some of the initial shock was wearing off (as one of my friends said to me, 'Married Woman Becomes Pregnant' is not making headlines anywhere) and I did enjoy a lot of the amazing sensations of growing a baby, not to mention the perks, like indulging in my love of Pop-Tarts.

There are a lot of things that pregnant women are advised against doing for the health and safety of their unborn baby – obvious things, such as giving up drinking and smoking and recreational drug use. But, in this modern age, the Internet has cooked up a whole host of other, seemingly innocuous activities, that are now considered verboten.

Now, if you're like me, a bit of a worrier (or catastrophist, as Himself says), then it'd be easy to get completely bogged down in all the shoulds and shouldn'ts of childbearing.

I went through an unfortunate phase, after straying onto an American pregnancy website, of agonising over whether or not I could have smoked salmon. Important side note: the Americans are (surprise, surprise) particularly hysterical about the eating habits of gestating ladies and must be ignored at all costs. So, here is my alternative list of pregnancy don'ts:

1) Do not Google any pregnancy-related issues.
2) After flouting rule number one (which you will, of course), do not entertain the Americans. American websites will inspire in you feelings of guilt and self-flagellation of epic proportions after doing something fairly innocuous like eating a piece of Parma ham.
3) First-timers – do not babysit while pregnant. Conniving family members will try to convince you that it'll be good practice to mind their babies while they, literally, run from the house to the nearest vodka tonic. Himself and I babysat our new baby nephew when I was about five months along and I was traumatised. The baby (who is adorable) cried for approximately 15 minutes – then I cried for the next four nights, wondering just what, just WHAT we had gotten ourselves into.
4) Do not watch films such as *The Conjuring* or *Prisoners* or *We Need to Talk About Kevin*, or Louis Theroux's documentary on the paedophile prison while pregnant. That one is pretty self-explanatory.

Now for some fun dos:

1) Do take advantage of the 'I'm carrying your unborn child' line – it literally applies to every scenario and is one hundred per cent effective at getting your own way.

2) Do draw a face on your bump when it gets sufficiently large. It'll look like a giant Mr Potato Head.

3) Do snuggle the bump up close to your partner in bed at night. This facilitates the baby in kicking its father repeatedly in the back. I understand that this is good for mother/baby bonding, and is essential in setting a precedent for the inter-familial ganging up – so important in later years.

4) Do gleefully ignore any coercive attempts to make you cultivate a maternity style. I'm so sick of women 'doing pregnant' well (I'm looking at you, insert Random Celeb Name here). Just accept the fact that you will most likely look like a boiled ham in a smock shirt for the duration, and console yourself with some delicious brown soda bread (see page 249) slathered in butter and jam.

As I've mentioned before, I have no sisters and, as of yet, none of the Bitch Herd has spawned, so when weird and wonderful things began to happen to me, I had no one to turn to but the Internet (bad idea) and Herself (worse idea).

During my first trimester I dodged a lot of unpleasant morning sickness, but I did have a lot of mysterious and very unpleasant pains. I was perpetually terrified that something was going wrong and sought reassurance from Herself. When I described my pains, she looked confused and said, 'My God, is that normal?'

Massively comforting, as you can imagine. I asked her what she had felt like when she was pregnant with me, to which she replied vaguely, 'I didn't show until I was at least seven months and I liked a bit of toast first thing in the morning before getting out of bed.' Didn't show until seven months? I kind of felt like slapping her.

Next I turned to Original Mrs White, my mother-in-law, for some sage words. She seemed to think that my giving up drinking was the height of eccentricity and promptly gave me a copy of *Everywoman: A Gynaecological Guide for Life*, which proved most unhelpful and contains these fantastic words of advice regarding weight gain during pregnancy: 'If an expectant mother gains more than 35lbs in pregnancy she will find it almost impossible to lose the extra weight. Her clothes will not fit and her former sylph-like figure will be a memory.'

Obviously there is not now, nor was there ever, anything remotely sylph-like about me. I also suspect that I may have gained the whole 35lbs in one sitting quite early on in the pregnancy when I made and consumed a mega sandwich of poached pears, Stilton and bacon. This sandwich can also be rebranded as a slightly classier starter if you omit the bread and arrange the elements on a plate with some baby leaves. As I was pregnant, however, I was not concerned with salads.

Along with all the glowing (sweating) and joy (hormones) of the human gestation, there is a fair bit of humiliation and embarrassment.

Your body is doing a range of new things that you have no control over. It is also the subject of frequent examination. Midwives performing scans might, for example, comment on how full your bladder looks – this is unnerving. Strangers will tell you you're carrying very low – why are they even looking down there and giving your pelvis this much thought? And, as the end goal is to safely carry and deliver your child, your dignity is not a priority. For anyone.

10 legitimately humiliating things that happened when I was pregnant …
1) I was the ridiculous woman who said to the doctor, 'I didn't even know you could get pregnant if you didn't have a period!' The doctor responded with an eye roll. He was lucky that hormones weren't strong in me yet.

2) I cried at work. Frequently.
3) I thought my waters broke in Tesco.
4) It turns out I pissed myself in Tesco.
5) I had to undergo THE COUGH TEST, an examination so humiliating for everyone involved that I didn't know who I felt more pity for – me or the student doctor who had to perform it.
6) I had a full-scale rant at yoga about the fact that they charged €3 extra for the prenatal yoga class. I think I shouted to anyone who'd listen, 'They're charging for foetuses now. It's a foetus-fee.' The hormones were strong in me at this point. I never went back there, not because of the rant but because ...
7) I farted in prenatal yoga. It was the worst.
8) I dropped my urine sample on the bus. The motion of the bus caused it to weave and roll away from me. I scuttled after it, desperately trying to retrieve it. A fellow passenger picked it up for me. It was still warm. And damp. 'From when I washed the container,' I tried to explain. In moments such as these, further explanation really only serves to compound the awkwardness. People were watching the encounter with great interest. I got off at the next stop.
9) I had to be rolled over by himself whenever I was lying down.
10) During the C-section, proceedings had to be halted while a nurse was dispatched to procure a razor. To shave me. Himself 'joke-thanked' the doctor. I was heavily medicated but through the morphine-haze could still sense that this was deeply embarrassing, not to mention inappropriate.

I thought I had shaken off the blackness that had settled on me during early pregnancy. But about three weeks before the baby was born I became plagued by profound anxiety. Like many heavily pregnant women, I couldn't sleep and spent my nights pacing the house.

Occasionally I would go and stand in the baby's room and look at the various newborn accoutrements we had amassed for our baby, and I would experience a terror so strong I would feel physically sick. A few times Himself had to come in and get me, sporting the unnerved look of a man whose wife appeared to have developed a bizarre phobia of the changing mat that said 'mama's little giraffe' on it.

Things that were totally benign, the tiny babygrows, the knitted caps, had taken on nightmarish proportions and I tried to avoid baby-related items as much as possible. Not easy when you're nine months pregnant. Also, I found there was this constant self-reflexive sensation of feeling the feelings, then worrying about what the feelings meant, and then worrying about worrying about what having the feelings meant. The anxieties were like a set of Russian dolls, each anxiety containing another even more acute terror about what the first terror might mean. Of course, it was all worryingly familiar to me.

The thought that, with my history of loopiness, becoming pregnant would pose certain issues for me had of course crossed my mind. It was one of the reasons why, prior to that, I had never been able to imagine actively deciding to become pregnant. Since recovering from the madness the most notable triggers for relapses were any kind of life change, even ones that on paper should have been happy events, such as getting married. It's fairly standard to feel anxious around big transitions, but I could usually tell if my reaction was on the normal spectrum or if it was tipping into mania. I've returned to my old counsellor a few times over the years when I'm having a wobble. The wobbles, by the way, for the most part ease out after a few weeks and usually feel like an attack of brain nausea and a bit of repetitive, negative thinking along the lines of 'It's back, I know I'll never be normal, I'll never shake this'. Going back for cognitive behavioural therapy top-ups has helped me though these times immeasurably. CBT is quite a logical and rational approach to mental disorders, which I find comforting. Dr Den would ask me to explain my repetitive thinking, what the focus of my fears were, and then tease out exactly why I was giving these thoughts such credence. When analysing the thought 'What if I kill my family?' he would, through questioning me, reveal that I didn't want to do this and, therefore, logically speaking, it was, we could agree, fairly unlikely that I would do it. That kind of thing.

When I became pregnant I was terrified that I would not be able to deal with the stress of being pregnant and that this would trigger a relapse worse then I'd ever experienced before. And, most unfortunately, this totally did happen in quite a protracted and insidious way over many, many months. Looking back on this period I am quite disappointed in myself, because this time I didn't go back to my doctor, when I needed to more than ever. With fairly uneducated hindsight I can only really guess at why I didn't recognise and act on the warning signs. I think that something people with no firsthand experience of mental illness find quite frustrating is understanding that the ill person's perspective is severely impaired. You're just not thinking straight.

As I said previously, for a good two or three months I felt quite good about being pregnant, but as the due date drew nearer I got sucked down into the hole. Pacing the house at all hours and refusing to engage with the baby stuff was not the behaviour of a well person. I was definitely experiencing obsessive thoughts, most of which centred around developing postnatal depression, an almost pathological conviction that I would not love or bond with my baby and a deep-rooted terror of not having a natural birth.

My son was breech in the womb and, after several failed attempts to shift him, I was booked in for a C-section. A few days before the appointed day I was called into the hospital due to irregularities in some blood tests performed because I am rhesus negative. The procedure was pushed up by several days and I was to have the baby that night. I was installed in the labour ward with a room of about 12 labouring women to wait for the operation. A backlog of C-sections meant that at the last minute mine had to be rescheduled for the morning and they sent my husband away. I was so frightened and alone for the next eight hours. I listened to a hypno-birthing CD and lay on the bed, silently racked with panic for the night. At 6.00 am they came to get me, demanding to know where my husband was and how soon he could get there. They told me to ring him and tell him to meet us up there and I felt physically sick at the thought of being cut open without him. This all probably sounds like a very First World problem, especially to women who have experienced traumatic labours, but there we are, this was a trauma for me. I'd read somewhere that C-sections were linked to increased chances of developing postnatal depression, so to my mind I was already fulfilling this prophecy.

As a final word on how irresponsible I was in relation to the whole not feeling very well in my head during the pregnancy thing, I never told any doctors or midwives about my history of mental illness. So that was pretty damn stupid.

STILTON, BACON, RED WINE AND POACHED PEARS SANDWICH

This is the epic sandwich that pushed me firmly away from that apparently sylph-like pre-pregnancy figure. As I said before, you can class it up by omitting the bread and making it a starter or light lunch. OR you can take it to bed with you one afternoon, watch *What About Bob?* and have, frankly, one of the best days of your life. Ever. You decide.

Side note: This sandwich is inspired by a sandwich in The Pepper Pot Café in Dublin's Powerscourt Centre, an alma mater of Himself's and purveyors of some of the nicest nosh in Dublin. **Makes 4 (or 4 starter salads, without the bread)**

- *600ml red wine*
- *300ml red wine vinegar*
- *125g clear honey*
- *300g caster sugar*
- *3 dried bay leaves*
- *3 whole star anise*
- *4 pears, peeled and cored, but left whole*
- *200g Stilton cheese*
- *150ml pouring cream*
- *½ teaspoon cayenne pepper*
- *8 bacon rashers*
- *8 slices good white bread*

Put the wine, vinegar, honey, sugar, bay leaves and star anise into a small saucepan over a medium heat and bring to the boil. Reduce the heat, then add the pears and arrange them so that the liquid just covers them. Simmer for about 30 minutes, or until the pears are tender. Using a slotted spoon, gently remove the pears from the pan.

While the pears are cooling, beat the cheese, cream and cayenne pepper together to a spreadable consistency. Heat a frying pan over a medium–high heat and fry the rashers. To assemble the sandwiches, spread the cheese mixture on 4 of the bread slices. Arrange two slices of bacon and a sliced pear on top. Top with the remaining bread slices and serve.

CHEWY QUINOA GRANOLA BARS

Frequently while pregnant I would find myself completely besieged by a hunger like nothing I had ever known before. Once I was at a concert, enjoying the vocal and comedic styling of my hero Loudain Wainright one minute, and the next minute, having abandoned Himself with barely a word of explanation, I was barging past the crowds on a demented hunt for anything, ANYTHING! to eat. I veered out of the venue, eyes wild, tongue hanging out slightly and hailed a taxi to take me to the nearest eatery. I was so crazed with hunger that I forgot I had actually cycled to the concert and left my bike locked to Himself's, which caused problems later. After that episode I never again left the house without these granola bars to feed the hungry foetus within. **Makes about 18**

- *225g rolled oats*
- *150g quinoa (rinsed in cold water and dried in a clean tea towel)*
- *75g pecan nuts, roughly chopped*
- *60g desiccated coconut*
- *125g pumpkin seeds*
- *15g coconut oil*
- *150ml clear honey*
- *150ml maple syrup*
- *75g dried cranberries*

Preheat the oven to 180°C/Gas 4, then line a 25.5 x 30.5-cm baking tray with baking paper.

Put the oats, quinoa, pecan nuts, coconut and pumpkin seeds into a bowl and mix to combine. Spread the mixture on the prepared tray.

Bake in the preheated oven for 15 minutes, stirring the mixture about halfway through cooking.

Put the oil, honey and maple syrup into a saucepan over a medium heat and heat, stirring, until the oil has melted and is well mixed in.

Transfer the toasted mixture from the tray to a large bowl and add the cranberries. Firmly stir in the warm liquid, making sure that all of the dry ingredients are well coated.

Line the tray with a fresh sheet of baking paper, turn out the mixture onto it and firmly press into the tray. Reduce the oven temperature to 150°C/Gas 2 and bake for 30–35 minutes, or until the top is golden. Leave in the tray until almost completely cooled, then carefully slide out onto a board and cut into 18 bars. Store the bars in an airtight container.

* The bars can be a little crumbly when you cut them, but you can keep the crumbly bits to use as a delicious topping for both yogurt and fruit.

BROWN SODA BREAD

When I was unable to sleep at night in the late stages of pregnancy I would lie among the fortress of pillows that our bed had become and think about warm soda bread dripping with butter and jam. That, or how terrified I was of just how this baby would be making an exit from my body through what is clearly a too-small passage. And how, when it was out, what on earth was I going to do with him? What if he hates me? What if I don't ever feel like a mother? What if he …? Draw breath. During these manic panicked ponderings I would always try to talk myself down with the thoughts of warm soda bread. Then, near dawn, when there was clearly no possibility of getting to sleep, I would get up and the bump and I would go down to the dark kitchen, turn on the radio and make bread. It was like an ad for life insurance, except for all the crazy worrying and the frankly grotesque gorging that would follow when the bread was out of the oven.

Makes 1 loaf

- *250g plain flour*
- *2 teaspoons salt*
- *15g bicarbonate of soda*
- *250g wholemeal flour*
- *75g jumbo oats*
- *2 tablespoons golden syrup*
- *350ml buttermilk*

Preheat the oven to 200°C/Gas 6.

Put the plain flour, salt, bicarbonate of soda, wholemeal flour and oats into a bowl and mix to combine. Make a well in the centre of the mixture and stir in the golden syrup and buttermilk.

Line a loaf tin with baking paper. Using your hands, bring the mixture together into a loose, wet dough and scrape it into the tin.

Bake in the preheated oven for about 35–40 minutes, or until the base of the loaf sounds hollow when you tap it with your knuckles.

Transfer the bread to a wire rack and leave to cool before serving.

CHAPTER 15

Food to eat while you are falling in love with your baby (and contemplating running ...

In which a hospital gives

me a baby to take home and I kind

of FALL APART.

... away〉

MY SON, YER MAN, WAS BORN THE WEEK BEFORE CHRISTMAS INTO A HECTIC operating theatre. Even under the thick blanket of anaesthetic I could feel the surgeon tugging on my insides moments before a strangled gurgle was heard. Himself, at my head, said in this quiet, awed voice, 'Did you hear that?' I was fully awake but when I tried to speak I realised how stoned I was because all I came out with was 'Is that my stomach? Because I'm hungry … '. He said, 'That's our baby.' Now he was smiling as the doctor lifted what looked freakishly like a wet, squirming, freshly skinned rabbit up over the little curtain thingy that had been erected to protect me from seeing the procedure.

I often think about how once a woman becomes a mother it must be hard for men to forget the montage of horrific images they are left with after the delivery room. When feeling amorous I always imagine Himself suddenly flashing back to that day and thinking (as I give him my best come hither look), 'I know what her organs look like.' Even worse for the men who have been present at a vaginal delivery.

After a quick glimpse at the rabbit thingy that looked kind of organ-like itself and was now emitting odd little squeaks, I was taken to recovery. This is a difficult aspect of a C-section – you have to go and wait in a room until the feeling comes back into your body, when all you want is to meet your baby. I lay there thinking about how the baby and I couldn't be getting off on a worse foot. On a rational level

I knew that this recovery time was a necessary step, yet I couldn't help but feel like I was already shirking motherhood somewhat. 'At least I have the morphine,' I thought, as the nurse gave me a little button to click when I wanted more. There was a timer on the device to limit patients to a hit every six minutes. 'That'll never do,' I thought for all of five seconds, until the first bit kicked in and I realised that, most unfortunately, I belong in that small percentage of people whose bodies don't actually like morphine. 'I thought morphine was the best,' I whined groggily to the attending nurse as she handed me a flimsy little Styrofoam hat to be sick in.

The hospital stay seemed to last forever. In reality it was only five days, but it is remarkable just how quickly you can become institutionalised. My abiding memory of hospital was feeling very frightened pretty much at all times and trying very hard to hide it. The anxiety and the fear seemed to be bubbling up inside me uncontrollably, about to spill over into my every transaction at any minute. I couldn't stop obsessing about how 'wrong' my reaction to becoming a mother was. How it wasn't 'normal' to be frightened of the baby and it wasn't 'healthy' to have to make yourself touch the baby. I felt queasy with anxiety and, once more, like I was observing myself and those around me at a remove, looking down the wrong end of the telescope at the scene in the ward.

The mothers in the beds around me seemed so genuinely happy, and I couldn't imagine what they were experiencing. I felt like running away. Genuinely running. I thought about how Herself and Himself and the baby would cope without me and I came to the conclusion that I couldn't dwell on this too much as running was actually a totally necessary bid for personal survival. 'They shouldn't take it too personally,' I figured. Plus, no mother was surely better than a crazy person for a mother, I reasoned. Once again, plotting my escape gave me some sort of relief.

Obviously on the surface of things I was engaged in one of my most committed impressions of 'everything is fine' that I'd attempted since the 'I might kill my family and I'm a little bit concerned that my arm is possessed' days. The very next day after my C-section I was up at 7.00 am, sitting on my already made bed waiting for the breakfast tray to come around. I wanted to be top of the class. The mad logic was definitely taking hold. 'I must not give in to the mental,' I obsessively thought 8,000 times an hour. 'I must put on make-up and get myself together,' was my pathologically cheerful internal refrain as I applied foundation. I was manic. 'Everything's great.' I smiled tightly and told anyone who asked, 'Everything's fine.'

The nights were very long and lonely in the hospital. Himself, along with the other dads, was sent home at 10.00 each night. While he was there I felt marginally calmer. He would read to me from the newspaper and I would remind myself that I was lucky. So, so, so lucky. Lucky that I wasn't caught up in a war zone or natural disaster. Lucky that the baby was healthy and lucky that I had him at all. But why, a niggling voice kept asking, did I need this reminding? Why couldn't I just feel it? What's wrong with me? I wondered. And will it ever be right?

I paced the rubber floors with a baby who woke at 1.00, 2.00, 4.00 and 7.00 am. I stared out of the hospital windows at the things I'd been looking at all my life and wondered why the world looked so alien. The warm little body slumped on my shoulder was my companion in this strange new world. I pointed out the Pigeon House – as for so many Dubliners a true landmark of my life, a beacon and a talisman, the view that means home and would now mean home for my son. I explained to him that the towers looked a little different from this angle. I pointed out Lansdowne Road and explained that I'd probably never get the hang of calling it the Aviva. I scanned the roofs of Irishtown and searched for the solar panels and bit of bright green piping that would alert me to the roof of our house, under which Himself was presumably sleeping, grinding his teeth with his eyes half open in that exceptionally creepy style of slumber that he has. I have possibly never felt more alone, yet in the same instance understanding that the little warm body meant that I would never be alone again. It was a realisation of that parental catch-22, that I would never be free, not because I couldn't run away, but because, no matter what, I would never want to.

During my stay in hospital having Yer Man, the Bitch Herd managed to breach the fortress of security that is the recovery ward and breezed in on a Sunday morning. They looked, to my morphine-addled and sleep-deprived mind, uncannily like the original supermodels. I'm talking Naomi, Christy and Cindy in the flesh.

Basically, they were all just wearing nice jeans and had blow-dried hair, but I was bowled over by their perfection. I, on the other hand, after three days of motherhood, looked like an old, wrung-out J-cloth.

If they were shocked by my appearance, they hid it well, cooed over the baby and then hightailed it before the burly head midwife could give out to them again. A few days later, one of them rang me at home to see how things were.

Let me add a visual context to this call. When she rang, I was lying on my bed staring at the wall. I'm not even sure where Yer Man actually was, presumably in the care of Himself, or some other person capable of picking him up without dissolving into hopeless tears.

'I don't know what I've done to my life,' I said in a blank voice that she barely recognised. 'So, it's not great?' she asked tentatively. 'No, not great,' I replied and hung up. Later, I realised that I had been too real with her that day. This is why nobody tells the truth about motherhood – we need others to join us. I had passed through to the other side and, until one of them joined me, I would need to protect them lest I scare them off procreating altogether. Post natal is referred to like it is a temporary state, but, really, it is one of life's watersheds. My mother is nearly 30 years post natal and claims to have still not recovered.

When I first searched for any feelings towards Yer Man, I found nothing, and this terrified me. Every day, I tried to practise and train for loving him. If you are a parent and this makes no sense to you, then you are one of the lucky ones.

Walnut Whips will always remind me of this time, because Himself would bring them home to me to cheer me up. In a kind of a detached way, I wondered at the fact that I needed 'cheering up' when I was clearly so lucky to have a healthy little baby in my arms.

10 times I kind of suspected that I had postnatal depression

1. When Himself first showed me the baby in the delivery room and I felt quite frightened, not of the magnitude of parenthood or anything, but actually frightened of the tiny creature, and then frightened of the very reaction of being frightened, which was surely not the right or natural way to be feeling.

2. When I felt like crying ALL THE TIME, but was too terrified to cry in case I literally never stopped. I had heard about the baby blues, and the phenomenon of crying all day on day three or four or 15, but to still be feeling this on day 168 was draining and so terrifying. I didn't allow myself to cry. I really tried to keep it in at all times. I felt paralysed, but I was also certain that if the crying started, it would never stop and I would cry for ever.

3. When I left my son with my mum in the hospital room to go and get a coffee. I skipped down to the coffee shop feeling temporarily free; then the strange giddiness subsided, replaced by a strong urge to be sick at the thought of him up there without me. In that moment, it hit me that this is the prison of parenthood. We will never be free. I abandoned the coffee order to get back up to his bedside, where he had lain blinking and perfectly serene since I'd left.

4. When, on the day I left hospital, a kind, very young and very wise midwife suggested that I go to the showers, turn on the water and scream and cry it out. I did this. It provided temporary relief from the strange feelings that were roaring inside me at all times.
5. When I felt petrified of being left alone with the baby, which, as the child's mother, is an unfortunate state in and of itself, but I was even more terrified of the fact that I was terrified. What did it all mean?
6. When my relentless quest to appear fine meant my hair and make-up were perfect at 7.30 in the morning. I was not fine. My friend came to see me and said, quite simply, 'You're in the hole.' Since then I have met others in 'the hole' and can now get a sense of how far I've come, but yeah, I think I was in the hole.
7. When even just displaying the baby cards from well-wishers was out of the question. Just encountering a powder blue missive exclaiming, 'It's a boy!' was enough to send me back to the bedroom with the blinds drawn. Himself put all the cards away in a box as and when they arrived, looking understandably perplexed, with the tiny baby lolling on a muslin square over his shoulder.
8. When I thought my son hated me. When I thought I hated my son.
9. When I spent Christmas morning staring at a wall and blankly wondering 'what have I done to my life?' and also, oddly, not really caring.
10. When I really, really felt nothing for my son. And hated myself for it. Every night I put him to bed and said, 'You're the best thing that ever happened to me', and willed myself to feel it.

I was never diagnosed with postnatal depression; I never sought professional help or medical advice. Himself and my mother were very concerned about me, but I wouldn't listen. I was obsessed with being fine. Fine. Fine. Fine. Fine. I was too scared to admit that something may not have been fine about how I was feeling. And I felt that I had no right to complain about my healthy baby and my charmed life when others were struggling so much.

I guess I eventually accepted that there are degrees of not fine, and all of it is okay to feel. With my background in Crazy, a big part of me felt that my bizarre reactions to parenthood were kind of inevitable. And even though I had come through very black times in the past, times when I was absolutely certain that I would be killing myself shortly, in the year after having my son I lost all perspective and couldn't believe that I would ever feel normal again. I didn't think I would ever get to the stage of feeling that I truly, madly adored my beautiful boy, but I have. Maybe I would've got here sooner had I accepted some help. Maybe not. Either way I got here. He's fucking deadly and I love him.

He's the best thing that ever happened to me.

HOME-MADE WALNUT WHIPS

Since then, I am glad to report that Yer Man is really growing on me – he's heaven. I compulsively smell his head and kiss his delicate little stem of a neck 82,000 times a day. He's an independent little toddler now who shrugs me off like I'm some overly attached girlfriend mis-calling him 17 times in a row. I have to steal the cuddles from him when he is distracted, which really compounds the feeling that I am his stalker. Since the early days of motherhood mania when Himself would bring me walnut whips to cheer me up, I have learned that, for me, walnut whips and babies have something in common. I like the ones I make myself the best. **Makes 24 mini whips**

- *400g plain or milk chocolate*
- *225g caster sugar*
- *100ml cold water*
- *12g powdered gelatine or 1 gelatine leaf*
- *50ml hot water*
- *1 egg white*
- *1 teaspoon vanilla extract*
- *cooking spray, for greasing*
- *24 walnut halves*

You will need:
- *2 12-hole silicone moulds (ice trays work well)*
- *a sugar thermometer*

Put the chocolate into a heatproof bowl set over a saucepan of gently simmering water, making sure that the base of the bowl isn't touching the water, and heat, stirring, until melted. Using a teaspoon, line the sides of your moulds with the melted chocolate and stand upside down on a sheet of baking paper to set, reserving some of the melted chocolate (keep it warm) to seal the tops.

Put the caster sugar and the cold water into a deep saucepan over a low heat and heat until the sugar has dissolved. Increase the heat to medium and bring the mixture to the boil. Resist the urge to stir. Place the sugar thermometer in the syrup and continue cooking for 8–10 minutes, or until the temperature reaches 120°C.

Meanwhile, dissolve the gelatine in the hot water. Place the egg white in a clean, grease-free bowl and whisk until it holds stiff peaks.

When the syrup is ready, remove from the heat and carefully add the gelatine. Even if this is quite set, it will melt down in the syrup. Carefully pour the sugar syrup into the egg white, whisking constantly on a low speed. Add the vanilla extract and increase the speed. Continue whisking for a further 10 minutes until thick and glossy.

Fill the greased chocolate moulds with the filling. Use the remaining melted chocolate to seal the top of the mini whips and pop a walnut half on top of each before the chocolate sets. The whips are ready to eat once the chocolate is completely set.

CAJUN SPICED COD WITH RICE AND BEANS

This is a really fast, simple dinner that is full of flavour. Plus I always feel vaguely moral and virtuous having fish for dinner. I have become particularly sold on speedy suppers since having my very own little human to care for. Without sounding too much like a working mum cliché I like getting home and spending the evenings doing my (much-lauded) dolphin impression, singing 'The Wheels on the Bus' and smelling my son's head (this is all pre-wine, I would like to point out) and not cooking a lengthy involved dinner that Himself and I will invariably have to speed-eat in 3 minutes, standing at the kitchen counter, between bathtime and bedtime. **Serves 4**

- 2 teaspoons cumin
- 2 tablespoons paprika
- 2 tablespoons dried thyme
- 2 teaspoons cayenne pepper
- 2 teaspoons salt
- 4–6 cod fillets
- cooking spray, for cooking

Salsa
- ½ red chlli, deseeded and finely diced
- ½ red onion, finely diced
- 2 tomatoes, finely diced
- handful of fresh coriander, roughly chopped
- juice of ½ lime

To serve
- rapeseed oil, for frying
- 1 red pepper, sliced
- ½ red onion, finely sliced
- 140g brown rice, cooked according to the packet instructions
- 400g tinned red kidney beans
- 150g Greek-style yogurt
- juice of ½ lime

Preheat the oven to 200°C/Gas 6. Line a baking tray with baking paper. Put the cumin, paprika, thyme, cayenne pepper and salt into a bowl and stir to combine, then coat the cod fillets with the mixture. Place on the prepared tray and spritz with a little oil. Bake in the preheated oven for 12–15 minutes.

Meanwhile, to make the salsa, put the chilli, onion and tomatoes into a bowl and stir in the coriander and lime juice.

Heat a little rapeseed oil in a frying pan and sauté the red pepper and onion until softened. Add the rice and kidney beans and stir-fry to heat through.

In a small bowl, mix the yogurt with the lime juice. Serve the cod with the rice and beans, a generous spoon of the fresh salsa and a dollop of the lime yogurt.

MOUSSAKA

Moussaka was a favourite of mine during the round-the-clock nursing stage of new motherhood. Any food that can be consumed one-handed is fairly key when your child is suctioned to your tit like an adorable parasitic twin for 20 hours in every 24-hour period. It also always brings me back to the months I spent studying in Athens in my early 20s. My friend and I were on a tight budget at that time and our lunch was provided free of charge at the college cafeteria. This led to a lot of moussaka thieving. I can say with some authority that pocket moussaka eaten cold, between two slices of bread, six hours later, is delicious. It may also be the very epitome of student food. Crème fraîche is the base for a good cheat's béchamel sauce. **Serves 4**

- *2 large aubergines*
- *4 tablespoons olive oil*
- *1 onion, finely chopped*
- *4 garlic cloves, finely chopped*
- *1½ teaspoons ground cinnamon*
- *1 teaspoon dried oregano*
- *500g fresh lamb mince*
- *2 tablespoons tomato purée, mixed with 150ml water*
- *150ml red wine*
- *400g tinned chopped tomatoes*
- *small bunch of flat-leaf parsley, chopped*
- *150g crème fraîche*
- *50g grated Parmesan cheese*
- *2 eggs, beaten*
- *½ teaspoon ground nutmeg*
- *salt and freshly ground black pepper*

Preheat the oven to 180°C/Gas 4. Line two baking trays with baking paper. Thickly slice the aubergines, lay the slices on the prepared trays and brush with half the oil and a little salt and pepper. Bake in the preheated oven for 25 minutes until they are tender and floppy. Do not switch off the oven.

Meanwhile, heat the remaining oil in a pan over a high heat and sauté the onion for a few minutes until softened, then add the garlic, cinnamon, oregano and lamb. Fry, stirring occasionally, until the lamb is browned all over. Pour in the diluted tomato purée, the tinned tomatoes and the wine and simmer for 20–30 minutes, or until the liquid is reduced. Season with salt and pepper and stir in the parsley.

Whisk the crème fraîche, cheese, eggs and

nutmeg together. Arrange about a third of the aubergine slices on the base of a small ovenproof dish, layer some of the lamb mixture on top, then repeat the layers with the remaining aubergine slices and lamb mixture.

Finish with a layer of aubergine slices, then spread the sauce over the top. Bake the moussaka in the oven for about 40 minutes until it is browned on top. Leave to stand for 10 minutes before serving.

CHAPTER 16

People and other things I've **NO PATIENCE** for since making a human (and other thoughts on motherhood)

In which I detail what PROLONGED SLEEP DEPRIVATION can do for a person (apart from making them a strong contender in a Keith Richards lookalike competition).

BECOMING A PARENT DEFINITELY MADE ME A REALLY BAD PERSON. IN THE SHORT space of time between bringing the baby home from the hospital and hitting my ninth consecutive day of no sleep I quickly came to loathe virtually everyone for no real reason whatsoever. I also discovered unequivocally that I am not morally opposed to murder, I'm just too tired to actually commit one. Here is a list, in no particular order, of things I no longer have any patience for since becoming a parent: people, interfering people, constricting clothing, joy, judgement, getting the glass over the bottle of wine in a restaurant, people writing open letters (particularly of the 'Dear Mom on the iPhone' variety), anyone (who's not me) moaning about feeling exhausted.

The discovery that we are capable of homicide couldn't actually come at a worse moment for us parents, because at no other point in our lives are we the target of so many infernal clichés. The clichés crept in slowly, starting with an older lady at a pedestrian crossing who asked me 'Is he good?', indicating Yer Man in the pram. 'Is she asking me if he is good or evil?' I wondered to myself. 'Well, he's okay … he cries a lot but I'm trying to convince myself that it's not malicious,' I told her, a reply that she didn't seem at all satisfied with. 'But does he sleep?' she persisted. I upped my ante on pressing the button at the lights and thought for a bit. 'Well, I thought that they didn't really sleep … at this stage.' She pursed her lips, took another look into the pram and announced, apropos of nothing, 'That child is cold.' This was my first introduction to what I like to call 'complete fucking strangers who know more about raising my child than I do'. It is maddening, but you can barely leave the house with the child in tow without inciting hectoring lectures on what you're doing wrong, how your baby feels and what they need (that you are not providing). Apparently this is a completely unavoidable side-effect of parenthood.

Becoming a parent is a dangerous intersection of events. One, you may actually start to believe that you are in possession of super powers. And, in a way, you are, what with the bringing forth of life and lactating. And two, you somehow start to see other people as deeply irritating and, frankly, surplus to requirement now that you're making your own people and all. It doesn't bode well for your being remotely civilised for the duration of your parenthood and explains, at last, why all our parents were such assholes.

Upon entering the much-hyped club of procreators I couldn't help but think that the joy of the whole thing has been wildly overstated. Some actually seem to experience powerful joy in having babies. I am feeling a little bit cheated in this department, as no 'joy' has really kicked in. But then part of me suspects that I am not a 'joy person' – maybe I am just too cynical for profound emotional responses. I mean, I really love Yer Man – he's ridiculously good fun and he makes me laugh, but I feel that expecting constant joy from the little fellow is putting far too much pressure on him.

Fact is, maintaining ongoing joy is exhausting and unrealistic; I'm over feeling bad about not feeling joyful. I need to point out that I am so grateful for my lovely boy, but, seriously, I found that first bit (0 to anywhere from 12 to 83 weeks) to be borderline hellish. In fact, about two weeks in I wrote myself a slightly hysterical letter and sealed it in an envelope across which I'd written 'To be opened in the event of considering another baby'. When the time came I toyed with reading it, and then got a bit spooked that Crazy Past Me would talk Current Me out of expanding the family, and so I tore it up. No one needs to be reading the uncensored, wild ravings of a woman who's been awake and attached to a baby for 11 days straight – it's a dark place not to be revisited.

You possibly won't find many parents willing to admit to all this and maybe they are just better people than I am, but since day one I've begun to suspect that society as a whole is feeding us a major line on the whole parenthood thing. Most specifically I blame the hot moms of Instagram. You know them, right? They've just squeezed out a perfect 7-lb baby, having presumably avoided the indignity of shitting themselves in a room full of strangers, and are now chronicling the deeply irritating joy on their Instagram accounts. I don't participate actively in social media, but if I did, my Instagram account of the early days of motherhood would probably inspire a mass elective sterilisation among would-be followers. I look at the hot moms and genuinely wonder where all the tears and despair and anxiety are. I know that for many there are possibly genuinely none, then again maybe they just don't want to admit it because, let's face it, society as a whole doesn't really seem to rate honesty when it comes to this subject.

I've been developing a theory that the human race as a whole is engaged in an elaborate piece of performance art that I have entitled 'Isn't It Heaven?' Social convention demands that I preface anything negative about parenthood with the qualifier that I really do love my son and that motherhood is a magical state of near-perfection. So here goes: I love my son and motherhood is a magical state of near-perfection.

Now, on to the real business. Why is it so unacceptable to speak the truth on this one? I'm pretty sure that 'Isn't it heaven?' is a thoroughly modern invention. In my grandmother's day the prospect of procreation was so inevitable as to be deemed unworthy of comment or deep consideration. For my mother the advent of a child was something to be virtually concealed in a professional setting, such was women's paranoia that an entire career could be undone with so much as a nod to the fact that such a seismic and fundamental shift as a baby had taken place. But perhaps it makes total sense for motherhood to have now evolved to a spectacular one-woman show of impossible beauty and exquisiteness, in so far as these days our every move from choosing our shoes to eating a plate of food has become something of a performance, thanks to the dogged pursuit of virtual likes and panda emojis.

'Isn't it heaven?' The first time someone said this to me as I held my two-week-old son I burst out laughing. Then I realised she was serious and I conceded, 'If by "heaven" you mean full-tilt torture interspersed with some happiness when the baby sighs in a cute way or gets up a wind, then, yeah, I guess it is heaven.' This was not the answer she expected or wanted. I was then admonished for not appreciating my baby and didn't I know how lucky I was when so many people couldn't have babies. This argument always irks me. I do feel deeply for people who cannot have much-longed-for babies, but I also resent being made to feel in some way responsible for this by snitty bitches who apparently have a scarily simplistic view of the world.

I firmly blame the 'Isn't it heaven?' charade for why parenthood came as such a violent, life-altering shock to me. The only person who dropped the act during my pregnancy was Herself. While everyone else patted (unsolicited) the bump, saying cosy, comforting things like 'It's the best thing you'll ever do' and 'You'll realise that you never knew what love was', my mother was hissing in my ear about how she often hated me when I was an infant and how she nearly threw The Baby (me) out a first-floor window when I was three months old.

That's how she always refers to my younger self, The Baby. I suppose this is a way of separating her beloved current daughter (me) from the contrary, domineering tyrant child who tortured her for the best part of a year (The Baby). She acts as though we are in no way related and it can often feel as though she is bitching about The Baby to me (The Baby) behind The Baby's (my) back.

Herself's reports of motherhood were so bad that I simply couldn't accept that it was going to be that awful. As you can see I come from a long line of apparently ungrateful bitches. Now I'm grateful for that bit of realism because the 'Isn't it heaven?' act is only serving to make women feel like they're doing it wrong when they don't fall instantly in love with the sometimes magical, sometimes head-wrecking state of motherhood.

'He's being such a dick today,' I told Himself when Yer Man was two weeks old and had been crying for virtually the entire time. 'Yeah,' he agreed as we resumed the unending cycle of feeding, winding, rocking and wondering just what the hell was he after?

'I don't think I love him,' I whispered to a friend a few weeks in.

'Of course you don't,' she exploded. 'You don't even know him yet. Right now all he's doing is feeding and crying. This early on, at best, you might feel fiercely protective towards him, but that's about it.'

I definitely felt more of an obligation to him at that point and it's hard to pinpoint for me when exactly the love kicked in. Luckily it did.

I have to say, though, that there are women who fall in love in the delivery room and for whom this chapter may make no sense whatsoever. Which is understandable; parenthood, as universal as it is, is also wildly subjective. There's a lot of talk about judgement around these days and I think at the root of it is this sense that parenthood is something so common that it should be unifying rather than divisive. But it is divisive, because seeking a definite answer and unanimous agreement on something as personal as how we raise our kids is impossible and, more importantly, it's not actually necessary.

Take breastfeeding, for example. If you are a mother and you have been anywhere near the Internet for the last few years, then most likely you have read something about your method of feeding your baby that pissed you off and made you feel judged. There you have it, regardless of what method we've employed, we've all felt it.

I just want to take this opportunity to state categorically that I promise, whatever you may think, that I am far too concerned with what I'm potentially doing wrong in my feeble attempts to parent, to judge you on yours. And, likewise, I know that you certainly can't summon the will to care about me either. I think a lot of this judgement is in our heads and we all need to get on with not giving a shit about what the woman minding her own business over there might think about how we choose to feed, water or clothe our babies. Pretty much unless someone is literally getting their infant tattooed, I think they're doing a great job. If you *are* getting your baby tattooed, then I admit it, I am judging you.

Looking back on the early weeks of parenthood, I find it hard to distinguish what part of my reaction was quite possibly a clinical issue and what part was just a natural response to what is basically an utter life-hijack on the part of babies. The only other event (during the natural course of things) that can so resoundingly upend our life is somebody dying, which is possibly a weird analogy, but there you have it, it's true. Acquiring a baby can (oddly) resemble the stages of grief. There's denial: 'My life's not going to change'; anger: 'Why won't he stop crying?'; bargaining: 'If he would just sleep for two hours, I'll never complain ever again'; depression: 'This will never get any easier/what have we done to our lives?'; and then, huzzah, acceptance. And not only acceptance but love. Big love. Quite honestly a love you never knew existed. A love so vast that you're not quite sure how there is even room in your body for it, though for me, however big the love there's still room for quite a lot of confusion, frustration and tiredness. Never forget the tiredness.

SALMON AND CORN CHOWDER

Being chronically under-slept for the best part of two years means that I constantly need to comfort eat to buoy the spirits. However, the prolonged state of being shattered means that I am unable to prepare anything too taxing, so these recipes are my go-to when I want something warming and nourishing without too much palaver.

Yer Man used to be a great sleeper. I can say that now, safe in the knowledge that there will be no karmic retribution. You see, he has since become a terrible sleeper. When he was a good sleeper I had sense enough not to broadcast this in case another mother should (quite justifiably) physically attack me or something. Then, one day, about five months in, I whispered to somebody that Yer Man had started sleeping through the night at six weeks. At that very instant, upstairs in his cot, his eyes shot open, black like the eyes of the shark in *Jaws*, and so began his reign of terror.

I met a woman recently who has a baby a couple of months older. Clutching at hope, I asked if she was having any issues in the sleep department. Her response enraged me so much I had to leave the vicinity immediately. 'No, not at all, I just got him into a routine really early on.' I wanted to scream, 'Do you think that I just rejected the notion of a routine outright??? Do you think I haven't tried every night to replicate the "bedtime" of the night before with a zeal bordering on fanaticism?' In the end, exhausted by my own rage and lack of sleep, I slumped home and did the only thing I could do in the circumstances – I comfort ate. This is a light version of a chowder, which is good, as my main motivation for eating chowder is the accompanying brown bread and slabs of butter. **Serves 4**

- *1 tablespoon olive oil*
- *4 shallots, finely diced*
- *2 carrots, finely diced*
- *2 potatoes, finely diced*
- *2 celery sticks, finely chopped*
- *2 garlic cloves, finely sliced*
- *230ml fish or vegetable stock*
- *2 bay leaves*
- *450ml milk*
- *150g tinned sweetcorn (drained weight)*
- *300g skinned salmon fillets, cut into small pieces and checked for small bones*
- *handful of flat-leaf parsley, roughly chopped*
- *salt and freshly ground black pepper*
- *brown bread and butter, to serve*

Heat the oil in a large saucepan over a medium heat. Add the shallots, carrots, potatoes and celery to the pan, cover and reduce the heat. Cook gently for about 10 minutes, stirring to prevent sticking. Stir in the garlic and cook for about 1 minute. Add the stock and bay leaves and bring to the boil, then reduce the heat and simmer for 10 minutes until the vegetables are cooked through.

Add the milk and sweetcorn to the pan, bring to the boil, then add the salmon and simmer for a further 5 minutes to cook the fish. Check the seasoning and add a little salt if needed. Remove the bay leaves and ladle the chowder into bowls.

Scatter over the parsley and add a generous sprinkling of pepper. Serve with really good brown bread slathered in butter.

KATSU CURRY WITH COCONUT CHICKEN

Katsu is traditionally a Japanese curry and I'll admit it, this recipe is all kinds of bastardised. So it's not authentic but it is delicious. The sauce itself is super tasty while also not being overly indulgent, and the coconut chicken is a nice alternative to the breaded variety.

Serves 2 greedy people and a grabby toddler

- 1 tablespoon olive oil
- 1 onion, roughly chopped
- 4 garlic cloves, peeled but left whole
- 2 carrots, sliced into 1-cm rounds
- 105g plain flour
- 1 tablespoon ras el hanout
- 600ml chicken stock
- 2 teaspoons clear honey
- 1 tablespoon soy sauce
- 1 bay leaf
- 1 teaspoon garam masala
- ½ teaspoon salt
- 80g desiccated coconut
- 2 skinless chicken breasts, each cut into 3 pieces
- 1 egg, beaten
- sea salt and freshly ground black pepper
- cooked rice and chopped fresh coriander, to serve

Preheat the oven to 180°C/Gas 4. Heat the oil in a heavy-based saucepan over a medium heat and add the onion, garlic and carrots. Sweat gently, covered, for about 20 minutes until soft and caramelised.

Add 30g of the flour and the ras el hanout, then gradually mix in the stock. Increase the heat and bring to the boil, then add the honey, soy sauce and bay leaf and simmer for about 20 minutes, or until the sauce has thickened. Add the garam masala and check the seasoning, adding salt and pepper, if needed. Use a hand-held blender to blend the sauce until smooth.

Put the remaining flour into a bowl and mix in the ½ teaspoon of salt. Place the egg in another bowl. Spread the coconut on a plate. Dip each chicken piece in the flour, turning to coat evenly, then into the egg and, finally, coat with the coconut.

Put the prepared chicken pieces on a lined baking tray and cook for about 20 minutes, or until golden and cooked through. Serve on a bed of rice with the sauce spooned over the top, sprinkled with fresh coriander.

COCONUT AND BERRY CAKE

I'd be the first to admit that I'm not the best baker in the world. And that is why I love this recipe so much. In the making of it, the mixture actually curdles as par for the course instead of through my own ineptitude. So if the batter looks a bit shit, you're doing the right thing. This is the kind of cake to bring to an under-slept mother, if you have one in your life right now. She'll appreciate it. What's more, she might just refuse entry if you come without cake. **Serves 8–12**

- *125g butter, softened*
- *210g caster sugar*
- *2 eggs*
- *150ml milk, soured with a squeeze of lemon juice*
- *255g self-raising flour, sifted (or plain flour mixed with 1½ teaspoons baking powder)*
- *60g desiccated coconut*
- *130g frozen berries*
- *icing sugar, for sprinkling*
- *crème fraîche, to serve*

Preheat the oven to 180°C/Gas 4. Line a 23-cm round springform cake tin with baking paper. Put the butter and caster sugar into a bowl and cream until pale and fluffy. Add the eggs one at a time, making sure that the first one is fully incorporated before adding the second.

Add the soured milk and remain calm – this curdled look is totally normal. Stir in the flour and the coconut until they are just mixed.

Add the berries and stir through quickly.

Spoon the batter into the prepared tin and bake in the middle of the preheated oven for 30–50 minutes. It is cooked when the top has a nice golden colour and springs back at a touch, or when a skewer inserted into the centre comes out clean. Leave to cool in the tin for 30 minutes, then unclip and release the springform.

This cake is so moist that I usually don't bother with heavy-duty icing – a dusting of icing sugar and a dollop of crème fraîche is all it needs.

CHAPTER 17

I think I've gotten the hang of this

(and other things I've mistakenly believed about parenthood)

In which my infant son
manages to get me to cop on long enough
to realise that I officially **KNOW NOTHING
ABOUT PARENTHOOD**, and he appears
to be willing to forgive me for it.

I WILL ADMIT THAT I'VE SPENT THE LAST FEW CHAPTERS DETAILING MY SHOCK at parenthood and generally not painting too positive a picture of the whole experience, and, while I stand by my earlier statements, I feel I should explain that through it all, Yer Man, the child, never felt like the enemy. I think I thought my crazy brain was the enemy more than anything. And in my sleep-deprived, possibly post-natally depressed state, people who most unhelpfully said, 'EVERY mother can breastfeed', were the enemy. As were a good few other totally intangible things like colic, tongue-tie, routines and tummy time.

When he was tucked away safely inside me I always thought of him as a little astronaut tethered by the umbilical cord and floating in a vast space. As he grew bigger and I felt more and more full of baby, he was like my little buddy who would occasionally poke an arm or a foot or an elbow out in response to my voice. I sang to him as I baked at work early in the mornings when there were just the two of us. During hectic service in the restaurant I would whisper to him, 'The people on Table 5 are dickheads'. We would cycle around Dublin with my knees stuck out to the sides trying to avoid the growing bump, though occasionally I'd fail and he'd give me a petulant little kick in retaliation.

The first day of his life on the outside was strange for about a million reasons (not least the morphine drip), but the biggest surprise was that I felt like I didn't really know this baby. 'Remember when we ate all those hot dogs and watched eight episodes of *One Born Every Minute* back to back?', I wanted to say. Nothing. No flicker of recognition. He was kind of like the cool guy blanking me at a party. That night we were left alone in our curtained cubicle together as the wails of the five other babies on the ward serenaded us. I was feeling pretty awful (see Chapter 15 for details) and the midwife came around to help me latch the baby on for his first feed. Afterwards, he went into a strange little blissed-out trance. He was milk-drunk, but because I had never seen anything like it before, I completely panicked and called the midwife back. 'Oh yeah, they do that,' she said nonchalantly. 'They do???', I marvelled. It was the first time it really hit me what a mysterious, precious little creature this was – a part of me and yet infinitely unknowable at the same time. Side note: A few minutes later I snapped a picture of the milk-drunk baby and sent it to my entire family, in-laws included, not noticing that my nipple was in the bottom right-hand corner.

Himself and I drove the baby home from the hospital the day before Christmas Eve and it was the most fraught 10-minute journey of my life. We were white-faced and in a state of shock. 'I can't believe they gave us a baby,' I said. 'I know, they haven't even seen the state of the house,' Himself replied.

That first night at home with your first baby is probably going to be the weirdest night of your life. When it came time to go to bed I actually rang Herself to ask where I should put the baby to sleep.

'Do you have a cot?' came the impatient reply. 'Um, the neighbours gave us a Moses basket.' 'Put him in there, so,' she advised.

As bizarre and confusing as the first few weeks are for us new parents, I often think about how traumatised the babies must be. From the comfort of their meat-cave they have suddenly been ejected into a world of harsh lighting and unpleasant draughts, and their entire survival is dependent on two jabbering, hormonal imbeciles. Terrifying.

I imagine he, too, was wondering just what the hell the hospital were thinking entrusting him to us.

'These people can barely fit a car seat,' he implores the nurse as we leave the hospital. 'And that one with the long hair has definitely been on drugs pretty much the whole time I've been here.'

After about a week of him being out and about I started to feel like Yer Man was more like my parasitic twin than my child, what with being latched on to me virtually round the clock. This also stemmed from the fact, I think, that we were both as clueless as each other. He'd gaze up at me from these dark black eyes as I struggled with the poppers on his babygrow and I'd say helplessly, 'I know, I don't know what I'm doing either.'

He has been my partner in crime since day one. Even when we're fighting – I gave him the finger once when he wasn't looking – he is still my buddy. And even as an infant he had a lot to teach me about, well, life. He's pretty advanced like that. Before he came along I was definitely languishing, both professionally and creatively, and while pregnant I certainly didn't expect to be making any great leaps on the career front, what with a baby to care for and chocolate digestives to eat. But when he came along, as well as giving me an insatiable appetite for smelling the heads of babies (mine, yours, that baby over there, any baby – just give me a goddamn baby to smell), he also gave me this incredible impetus to get my shit together. Or to try, at least. I couldn't claim that the shit is together, though after two years of parenthood I have earned outstanding achievements in the field of excrement and I think I'm certainly a shade closer.

A year on from possible postnatal depression I've finally started to have so much fun with Yer Man. I have regrets about the kind of mother I was to him at the beginning, but I think he gets it and he's forgiven me. He's cool like that, and he knows me pretty well. Anyway, he seriously owes me. I gave him life and he's been pretty harsh to me at times. In the bath recently he picked up my sad, defeated boob and said, 'Moo!' Which was admittedly pretty clever (and accurate, sadly).

That's the moment of parenthood that even I will concede is magical, that day when suddenly your child not only walks and talks and feeds himself and plays with his toys and runs to give you a hug, but that moment when he makes a joke for the first time. Yer Man, I'm pretty sure – and this is no overstatement – may well be the funniest baby of all time. I've even heard him laugh in his sleep. He is an absolute craic-merchant, though sometimes his humour takes on a noticeably darker slant: One day I was reading an article about Joseph Fritzl and he pointed to his picture and said, 'Dada'.

Apart from his wit, Yer Man also possesses an innate contrariness that is quite possibly an inherited trait. Currently he is in that domineering phase where every question I pose is answered with 'NO', and this odd little commanding salute that makes me thankful he can't say 'Sieg Heil' yet. 'Do you want chocolate?' 'Sieg Heil,' he storms with his tyrannical salute. O … kaaaay, no to chocolate? This is around the point that I wonder if he is definitely my child. The C-section was pretty surreal, what with the no pushing and the little curtain thingy. I did kind of suspect that maybe they had a basket of babies down there at the end of the bed and just picked whichever one most closely resembled Himself and me.

Of all the profound lessons that motherhood has taught me about our capacity for love, our tolerance for touching another person's poo and how good babies' heads smell (seriously, it's almost edible), I think the most surprising thing I learned was just how crazy good at animal noises I am.

Seriously, nothing could've prepared me for how good my dolphin impression was going to be. It's like living your entire life never realising that you are actually a really good unicyclist or a contortionist. I also never thought that I would be so comfortable with doing the animal noises while out in public and yet, there I am, wandering the aisles of Aldi, going 'EEeeeeeeee, EEEEEEEHHHHH' to the child's delight, wondering what people are looking at. Then I remember that perhaps not everyone is accustomed to hearing such an exceptionally realistic dolphin impersonation.

I often wonder if Yer Man will ever read any of the things that I have written down about him. I'm banking on the Internet having imploded by the time he thinks to Google my name and finds an article I wrote entitled 'Ten sexual positions only parents will know'. If not he will have unending ammunition against me for the rest of his life. Should he, for example, become embroiled in a life of crime, you know how they always blame the parents? Let's just say the defence team will have all the legwork done for them and it'll be an open-and-shut case.

If by any chance he is reading this, I'd just like to say in response to any criticism that you may have regarding my representation of your early life, 'I breastfed you, you little bastard.'

And I love you.

BAKLAVA

As much as Yer Man is my absolute pal he is also more than capable of sabotaging me in that maddeningly cute and conniving way of all children. As a baby, his resources for retaliation are somewhat limited, but one method he used to employ to punish us was what we called the Mystery Sick. This is when you know that the baby has sicked on you but you can't for the life of you find it. The law of parenthood is that the elusive Mystery Sick will only ever show up later when in company or at work. When I finally find it (usually down my sleeve or back) after a colleague has asked me what it is, I always think to myself, 'Damn, he's good.'

As I find that the predominant sensation of parenthood is one of stickiness I thought it would be apt to include this recipe for my favourite, stickiest sweet treat of all time. Also, one time I bought a huge bottle of rosewater for a failed ice cream experiment and have used this as an excuse to make these baklava almost weekly ever since. **Makes 25–30 pieces**

- 12 sheets filo pastry (keep these under a damp tea towel during the preparation)
- 225g unsalted butter, melted, plus extra for greasing
- 300g mixed pistachio nuts and pecan nuts, roughly chopped
- 2 tablespoons caster sugar
- 1 teaspoon ground cardamom (or the crushed seeds of 10 pods)

Syrup
- 350g caster sugar
- 300ml water
- 2 tablespoons rosewater
- 1 tablespoon lemon juice

Preheat the oven to 180°C/Gas 4, then grease a baking tray. I use a tray that is roughly the same size as my filo pastry sheets (about 30 x 35cm).

One by one, place 6 sheets of filo pastry in the prepared tray, brushing each one with melted butter as you do so.

In a mixing bowl, combine the chopped mixed nuts, sugar and cardamom and spread this mixture evenly over the top sheet of filo pastry.

One by one, place the remaining sheets of filo pastry over the layer of nut mix, remembering to brush each sheet with butter as before.

With a sharp knife, make a criss-cross pattern on the top sheet as a cutting guide. Bake in the preheated oven for 20 minutes until the pastry is puffed and golden, then reduce the oven temperature to 140°C/Gas 1 and bake for a further 20 minutes.

Meanwhile, make the syrup. Combine the sugar, water, rosewater and lemon juice in a saucepan and bring to the boil. Reduce the heat, then simmer for 20 minutes until a syrup forms.

Remove the baklava from the oven and pour the syrup over the top and into the incisions. Leave to cool before cutting.

CHICKEN AND CHESTNUTS WITH CREAMY CIDER AND DILL

For those times when you're sick of cooking in wine, cider can bring much to the flavour party. Also, randomly, whenever we have a house party I find there's always one rogue bottle of cider left lying around for some reason and my motto is, if you can't stand to drink it, cook it. Or, if you happen to like cider, drink it while cooking with it. This is a very nice autumnal dish, creamy without being cloying. Keep the sides simple: some garlicky fine beans and boiled potatoes would be perfect. **Serves 4**

- *25g butter*
- *2 tablespoons olive oil*
- *4 skinless chicken breasts*
- *125g flour, seasoned with salt and pepper*
- *250g mushrooms, quartered*
- *250g cooked chestnuts, roughly chopped (optional – they're not that easy to find)*
- *500ml cider*
- *150ml double cream*
- *generous bunch of dill, chopped*
- *salt and freshly ground black pepper*
- *2 handfuls of toasted flaked almonds, to garnish*

Heat the butter and oil in a medium-sized deep saucepan. Roll the chicken breasts in the seasoned flour, then add them to the pan and cook until browned all over. Remove from the pan and set aside, then add the mushrooms to the pan and cook until softened. Add the chestnuts, if using, and the cider. Scrape any bits of chicken from the base of the pan with a wooden spoon.

Return the chicken breasts to the pan and bring to the boil, then reduce the heat and simmer for 30–40 minutes. Remove the chicken breasts from the pan. Increase the heat and cook the sauce for 5–10 minutes until reduced. Remove from the heat. Stir in the cream and dill and add a little salt and pepper if required.

To serve, spoon the sauce over the chicken and garnish with the almonds.

CONCHIGLIONI WITH BUTTERNUT SQUASH, BLUE CHEESE AND CRISPY SAGE

This is the meal that finally convinced the baby to give real food a go. He was so wedded to his liquid diet I had begun to fear that he would grow up and never surrender the bottle, that perhaps he would be on the milk forever. 'Maybe he won't ever be an eater,' I wailed to anyone that listened. That's just what new parenthood does to a person, it makes you a compete catastrophist. There are just so many things to agonise over, and as each 'issue' resolves itself another invariably presents itself. Right after the eating fretting came, ironically enough, the biting fretting. Yer Man's biting phase lasted about three weeks, but for those three weeks I was like a demented person. Was this a sign of some deeper psychological problem? What had I done wrong? Had some other baby bitten him? Is that where he learned it? Should I get a tetanus shot? Should I bite him back? Mad stuff. About a week later I moved on to worrying about willy pulling and forgot all about the biting until a friend mentioned that her one was at it.

While the crispy sage in this pasta dish is the total star of the show, the whole plate is an ensemble cast of delightful tastes and textures. It's as though Robert Altman himself directed. Using the Parmesan rind to add flavour during cooking also works well for soups. **Serves 4**

- 1 butternut squash, peeled, deseeded and chopped into 1–2-cm cubes
- olive oil, for cooking
- Parmesan cheese rind (optional)
- 4 garlic cloves, sliced
- ½ white onion, chopped
- 500ml vegetable stock
- 26 sage leaves
- 1 red chilli, sliced

- 250g dried conchiglioni (or any large pasta shells)
- 1 tablespoon chopped fresh rosemary
- 2 tablespoons crème fraîche
- 160g blue cheese, crumbled
- handful of pecan nuts, toasted
- salt and freshly ground black pepper

Preheat the oven to 200°C/Gas 6. Place half the squash on a baking tray, season with salt and pepper, add some oil and toss to coat. Roast in the preheated oven for 25–30 minutes, tossing occasionally, until golden and tender.

Place the remaining squash in a medium-sized saucepan with the cheese rind, if using, the garlic and onion, then pour in the stock to cover. Simmer for 25–30 minutes until the squash is soft and the stock has been partly absorbed.

Meanwhile, heat 2 tablespoons of oil in a frying pan over a medium heat, then add 20 of the sage leaves – they will flatten and darken. Take care not to burn them. Turn the leaves individually, then remove them from the pan and place them on kitchen paper to dry and crisp up.

Add the chilli to the pan and toss for a few minutes, then remove from the pan and set aside. Cook the pasta in a large saucepan of boiling salted water until firm to the bite. Drain and rinse.

Chop the remaining sage leaves. Remove the cheese rind from the squash and stock mixture and add the chopped sage and rosemary to the pan. Blend with a hand-held blender until smooth. Stir in the crème fraîche and add a little water to thin the mixture if necessary. Add the pasta and heat gently over a medium heat.

Divide the pasta and roasted squash between two bowls, then scatter over the blue cheese, sliced chilli, nuts and crispy sage leaves. Serve immediately.

APPLE FRITTERS WITH MINCE PIE ICE CREAM

Here is a dessert that is one part total palaver and one part ridiculously easy. I think they probably cancel one another out to be, as a whole, fairly doable. This is the only ice cream recipe you'll ever need in life again: no ice-cream maker required, no constant stirring by hand, no effort whatsoever. You can play around with flavour combos too. As for the fritters, yes, deep-frying is a pain in the ass – it must be an evolutionary thing to keep us from doing it too often (I hear it's not the healthiest). But, my God, a freshly fried fritter is worth the hassle, dammit.
Makes about 25 fritters and 10 portions of ice cream

- 250g plain flour
- 75g sugar
- 2 teaspoons cinnamon
- 2 teaspoons baking powder
- pinch of salt
- 150ml milk
- 2 eggs
- 2 tablespoons butter, melted
- 2 cooking apples peeled, cored and diced into 1-cm cubes
- 400ml sunflower oil
- 75g sugar mixed with 1 teaspoon cinnamon, for coating

Ice cream
- 200ml tinned condensed milk
- 4 tablespoons maple syrup
- 500ml double cream
- 8 tablespoons mincemeat

Make the ice cream the night before. In a bowl, combine the condensed milk and maple syrup. Whip the cream until it holds soft peaks. Gently fold the cream into the condensed milk mixture, stir in the mincemeat, then pour the ice cream into a plastic container and freeze. No churning needed – it really is the easiest ice cream ever.

To prepare the fritters, combine the flour, sugar, cinnamon, baking powder and salt in a bowl. Whisk the milk, eggs and butter together in a separate bowl, then gently mix the wet ingredients into the dry ingredients, ensuring that there are no pockets of flour.

Stir in the apples to make a chunky batter. Pour the oil into a saucepan and heat over a medium–high heat. When a small bit of batter sizzles and immediately rises to the top when dropped into the oil, it is hot enough. Drop tablespoons of batter into the oil and cook in batches of three or four, reheating the oil between batches. Cook the fritters for about 4 minutes, turning halfway through, then carefully remove and drain on kitchen paper. Toss the fritters in the cinnamon sugar and serve with the ice cream.

The fritters can be made up the night before – cook all the batter, drain the fritters, arrange on a lined baking tray and store overnight at room temperature. When you're ready to serve, preheat the oven to 200°C/Gas 6 and heat the fritters for 8–10 minutes until hot and crispy.

CHAPTER 18

Why I can't remember my father

In which I put up a pretty convincing
(I think) CASE FOR EUTHANASIA and
tell a story about Alzheimer's disease that
you've perhaps never heard before (hint: it's
nothing like the goddamn *Notebook*).

MY DAD WAS DIAGNOSED WITH ALZHEIMER'S DISEASE WHEN HE WAS IN HIS 50s, though the first sense that something was up was probably earlier. I remember that he was going to have a head scan to check if there were tumours or anything sinister on his brain as he had been forgetting things. I was at my 21st birthday party in my parents' house and that night we had virtually the only conversation we've ever had about his illness. I said something like 'I hope your brain is okay.' Frustratingly, I can barely remember his response.

That's a funny thing with Alzheimer's, and I wonder if it's something everyone experiences. Almost in direct proportion to how they are losing track of their own lives and memories, you, their devoted family and friends, are also forgetting who they are. My theory is that when someone you love dies your memory of them becomes incredibly sharp and it crystallises. But with Alzheimer's they are not gone, but they are gone. There is no ceremony or ritual that allows you to organise and frame your memories. Their continued existence somehow wipes out the memories of them before the illness. If I try to call him up as he was when I was a child I find that my thoughts are hijacked by the later versions of him.

Now, the very strongest memories that I have of my dad are not good ones. I remember the strange looks he would give me during a period when he was, we later discovered, suffering psychosis. He was standing in my hallway and refusing to come further into the house. I was holding my young son and remember feeling no concern, just frustrated and fed up. I try to think of my wedding day, but I can barely remember him being there. My mother made the speech and he sat by smiling. I try to remember him taking my hand to lead me down the aisle, but instead I am assailed by an unwanted memory from much later of him grabbing my hand and trying to bite it.

It feels like a terrible betrayal to not remember what a brilliant man he was, and even more of a betrayal to write these words here about what he became after the illness took over. But I am writing them because he deserves what he suffered to be known. To downplay it and pretend that what happened to him is anything less than catastrophic would be doing him and everyone like him a disservice. Also, I'm just really sick of the dementia narrative that makes it seem like it is the natural way of things, a gentle decline on the way to going quietly into the fucking night. Maybe it's like that for a lucky few, but the reality is that it is brutal. Alzheimer's is the blackest terror, it is the most alone and trapped and frightened you can be. It is one's memories, one's only proof of life and love and existence becoming liquid and slipping through your fingers faster than you can try to hold on to them. He has been robbed. He's been robbed of the chance to experience his wife and daughter and grandchild, of the chance to look back on his life and his work and feel a sense of achievement. He's been robbed of comfort and dignity and every pleasure imaginable. And still he has to live through it all. I am angry for what happened to him. He was not. He never seemed angry or upset. He was full of grace.

We hate to look too closely at illness but so many of us are looking at it every single day and it is so hard to understand why, with all of our compassion and belief in human rights, we can't fight for our right to die.

'I want him gone,' I told my friend, pissed at a wedding a few years ago. At that time he was still living in our family home and becoming more and more unmanageable. I told myself that it was a desire to end his suffering, but in reality I just wanted my own to end. A few days later and I had my wish in a sort of way. Himself and I had gone out for dinner, leaving the baby with my parents. When we arrived back at their house a couple of hours later there was a strange atmosphere. A few of my mother's friends were sitting at the kitchen table but no one was speaking. The baby and my dad were not around. As soon as we arrived the friends got up to leave with barely a word. It transpired that he had attacked my mother. He was still a fit man, tall and very strong. She managed to fend him off and somehow protect herself and the baby. She alerted her friends, who arrived within minutes, and one of them, a doctor, administered a sedative and put my dad to bed.

With dementia and Alzheimer's the only thing we thought we could count on was that the degradation would be slow, and I suppose I thought that however upsetting it would be, it would also be gentle. Like *The Notebook* or something. I didn't realise that it could also be swift and violent and that a person's soul could be snuffed out so fast, like a light being switched off.

It was hard to process this bizarre development. The thought of him hurting anyone, much less the woman that he had been devoted to since he was 16 years old was inconceivable. Everything seemed so skewed, tilted and out of control. We were all afraid of him. And yet there was also a strange kind of banality to the situation. We huddled in the guest room debating what to do.

'We can't sleep here,' Herself said, 'but we can't leave him alone.'

'He'll stay and we'll take the baby to my house,' I replied, volunteering Himself.

'But what about the knife?' she shot back.

'What knife???'

It was at that point that Herself announced that apparently all through their marriage, my parents had kept a large kitchen knife under the bed in case of intruders. Himself looked at me as if to say, 'And you think my family are crazy?'

My mother and I took the baby to my house while Himself spent the night locked in the guest room of my parents' house. My mother and I lay in my bed unable to sleep. Though we were in another house we still felt oddly vulnerable. In the dark of my bedroom I said, 'It's like I'm afraid he's going to come here and find us.' She also seemed fearful. Which, in and of itself, was utterly shocking, that we should be fearful of the man who loved us more than life. What a bullshit disease it is.

The next day my mother had him committed to a psychiatric ward. In a bit of bitter bureaucratic irony, he was too young to be admitted to the dementia ward. We didn't really know what else to do. As the years had passed since his initial diagnosis and his condition had steadily worsened we had adopted complete and utter denial as our stance on the matter. We never even mentioned the word Alzheimer's. We occasionally referred to Kev's 'memory problems', though never really to anyone beyond the immediate family. The whole Alzheimer's thing seemed like something that didn't really have anything to do with us. His 'memory problems' were more pesky than anything sinister.

After the diagnosis, the dynamic of our family had subtly changed, however. My mother and I were always close but we became even closer, and she would tell me each day of new manifestations of Kev's illness. It started to feel a bit like she was telling tales on him, but I understood why she felt the need to ring me and tell me that he had come down to breakfast wearing gloves but no shoes or socks. She needed someone to bear witness to the thing. She needed to mark his deterioration in some way. She needed someone with her to watch him go, and because we hadn't really told anyone else, that someone was me.

The denial strategy was ultimately a fairly terrible idea. It meant that when my dad lost all connection to reality and attacked my mum we were completely unprepared, either emotionally or practically. If I had spent so much as five minutes Googling 'early-onset Alzheimer's', I would have learned that psychosis is a common stage in the advancement of the illness and perhaps would've read the signs better. We might also have started the process of looking for a suitable home for him, a process we could even have included him in, perhaps.

I'm pretty sure that he wouldn't have gone in for that, though. I don't think my parents talked much about his illness even amongst themselves. I think this was mainly Kev's doing. His response to his slowly and quietly losing his mind was very clever. He became a master of appearances. In group situations he was adept at appearing engaged. He would laugh at what he thought were the appropriate moments and could fluff his way through encounters with vague responses and smiling and nodding.

In what was quite a bizarre reaction I would seethe internally every time I heard his fake laugh. He had always been so sharp and funny, and I don't know why, but I felt annoyed with him for losing that. Totally irrational, but I suppose when we are losing someone we all need someone to blame and I blamed him. I blamed him for refusing to talk about what was happening to him. For pretending he was fine, until he was so not fine that we were hiding from him. I blamed him for how guilty I felt, because eventually being around him was an obligation and not a pleasure. I blamed him for all the things that really were not his fault. I also kind of blamed my mother for good measure. And myself.

Now I feel a terrible shame about not cherishing him enough back then when he was lucid enough to know who I was. I always wondered if I am somewhat lacking in empathy. All I know is that I started to disengage from him at some point, perhaps as a form of self-preservation, and I feel pretty fucking bad about that now that it's too late.

Kev lives in a home now and I go see him once a week. And I hate it. It's not a bad place and the staff are incredibly kind. I honestly don't know how they do the job they do. He doesn't respond to us any more, his eyes are blank and unfocused and his face is becoming distorted because his head is constantly bowed, chin to chest. If I let myself think of him as he was even two or three years ago, I feel physically sick from the shock. His deterioration was so fast and so final and so devastating and so, so unfair. He is 63 years old, and he deserves to die because what he has is not living. It is no life at all. If I were braver I'd kill him myself. I hope someone would do that for me. We talk about it from time to time, Herself and I. It's unlikely to happen, particularly as I've now committed this to print. Also, as she points out, I have a young son, and being incarcerated would be a terrible inconvenience. Instead we're left waiting for the phone call that will end all this. I'm looking forward to the day when I can tell my dad goodbye and I love you.

EGG SANDWICHES À LA KEV

Food is something that gave Kev pleasure even up until a few years ago. Taste and smell are powerful forces. They can cut through the laws of physics and turn us into time travellers. A bite of lobster with the sea air tickling my nose brings back my dad, sporting that spectacular tan and a Panama hat, tucking into his annual lobster dinner on holidays in Spain. There's lots of foods that I associate with him; pungent cheeses, rich red wines, Bovril, weirdly (is it even food?), Yorkshire puddings, satsumas, chocolate, chocolate and more chocolate. He was a joyful eater and he loved cooking. His mastery of the notoriously tricky Christmas dinner, with its rigorous schedule of timings, was legendary.

The humble egg sandwich probably doesn't make it into a lot of cookbooks these days, but it would still make it onto the 18-course tasting menu that I hope to spend my last few hours on earth eating. I just adore the simplicity of the thing. My dad was a wonderful liar and, as a result, I grew up thinking that the egg sandwich was his unique creation. Obviously, as the years passed I spotted the ubiquitous egg mayonnaise virtually everywhere that food is served and concluded that once again I'd been had. His amendments to the egg sandwich were possibly not as innovative as he thought, but they are delicious; though, really, when has adding crispy bacon to something ever *not* been delicious? For a bit of added value I'm including my recipe for home-made mayo here so that the recipe isn't a total piss-take and delivers a touch more knowledge than simply 'mash boiled eggs with mayonnaise'.

Mayonnaise is a divisive little bugger. No one can agree on the single 'proper' way to make it and I can't say I've agonised too much over it. Some people add the acid at the end – I don't. So sue me. **Makes 1 large jar of mayonnaise and enough egg mixture for 2 sandwiches**

Mayonnaise

- *2 egg yolks*
- *1 tablespoon lemon juice*
- *1 garlic clove, crushed (omit the garlic if you are using the mayo for egg salad)*
- *1 tablespoon wholegrain mustard*
- *200ml olive oil (If the flavour of olive oil is too strong for you, use rapeseed oil or a mixture: 180ml rapeseed oil with 20ml olive oil at the end.)*
- *salt and freshly ground black pepper*

Place the egg yolks in a bowl with a good pinch of salt and whisk together vigorously until slightly thickened. Add the lemon juice, garlic (if using) and mustard and whisk until fully incorporated.

Slowly trickle in the oil, whisking constantly. You can't rush this part – any heavy-handedness with the oil and the mixture might split. When all the oil has been incorporated check the seasoning, adding a little salt or pepper if needed.

Kevin's Special Egg Mixture

- *2 eggs*
- *2 dessertspoons mayonnaise (see above)*
- *pinch of salt*
- *½ teaspoon cracked black pepper*
- *2 spring onions, finely chopped*
- *½ tomato, deseeded and finely chopped*
- *2 cooked bacon rashers, chopped*
- *Jacob's cream crackers and Campbell's cream of tomato soup, to serve*

Boil the eggs for 8 minutes, then leave them to stand in cold water for 10 minutes. Peel the eggs and mash them in a bowl with the mayonnaise, salt and pepper.

When well combined, mix through the spring onions, bacon and tomato. Serve on cream crackers alongside a bowl of Campbell's cream of tomato soup for some culinary time travel.

CHOCOLATE POTS

For the recipes inspired by my dad, I couldn't not include something chocolatey. Chocolate was like his life force. Ordering dessert in a restaurant was no hardship for Kev – he would just scan the list for the word 'chocolate' and, without further investigation into the dish, would simply point and order. I get my embarrassing penchant for hiding bars of chocolate from him also. Whenever Himself unearths a cachet of sea salt dark chocolate and duly mocks me, my defence is always that it's an hereditary trait. **Serves 6**

- *410ml single cream*
- *200g plain chocolate, broken into pieces*
- *2 teaspoons instant coffee*
- *2 tablespoons whiskey or coffee liqueur*
- *1 egg*

Pour 300ml of the cream into a saucepan and gently heat until just bubbling. Remove from the heat, carefully add in the chocolate pieces, then whisk together to melt the chocolate and combine it thoroughly with the cream. Whisk in the coffee and whiskey.

At this point, have a little taste to make sure the booze levels are to your satisfaction. Leave to cool to room temperature, then whisk in the egg. Pour the mixture into little glasses. I use quite generous shot glasses but small tumblers or espresso cups also work.

Place on a tray, cover with clingfilm and chill in the fridge for at least 6 hours until set.

Whip the remaining cream until it holds soft peaks, then spoon into the glasses. Serve with the biscotti on page 315.

BISCOTTI

These are great to serve alongside the chocolate cups or a cup of anything, really. They also make a lovely gift. They keep for about a week in an airtight container.

Makes 30 large biscotti

- *400g plain flour, plus extra for dusting*
- *250g sugar*
- *1 teaspoon baking powder*
- *zest of 1 lemon*
- *1 egg yolk*
- *3 eggs*
- *115g roasted hazelnuts*
- *150g chopped dried dates*

Preheat the oven to 180°C/Gas 4. Line a baking tray with baking paper. Put the flour, sugar, baking powder, lemon zest, egg yolk and eggs into a food processor and blitz to a sticky dough.

Turn out the dough onto a work surface lightly dusted with flour and knead in the hazelnuts and dates. Shape into a long flat loaf, place on the prepared tray and bake in the preheated oven for 35–40 minutes.

Leave to cool slightly, then cut into 1-cm slices and arrange on two baking trays. Switch off the oven and place the trays inside overnight to allow the biscotti to dry out and become crunchy.

CHAPTER 19

All about my

mot

In which I meditate on the CLAUSTROPHOBIC RAGE-LOVE of a mother and daughter and how, despite her obsession with my not separating delicate whites from non-delicate whites, I have still not murdered her in her sleep.

her

OBVIOUSLY I SHOULD PREFIX THIS WHOLE CHAPTER WITH: I LOVE MY MOTHER.

Moving on …

Every now and then, in a particularly maudlin moment, usually after leaving my father in his tortured existence as a prisoner of his own mind, my mother might utter the words …

'Why couldn't it have been me?'

And I find myself (privately) taking a little moment to, well, agree. Imagine this scenario. Imagine, I think, of a different reality where it was her instead of him stuck vacant and impassive in that chair. A reality where I could do something as insignificant as not wear lipstick and it would go totally unnoticed. I could come and tell her all my news and it would not be analysed and picked over and critiqued as though the future of the nation relied on whether or not I could get my act together and start separating non-delicate whites from delicate whites in the wash.

We could have this incredible relationship of tolerance, love and mutual respect, if only she were in a state of advanced dementia. Instead she is way too full of life for my liking. And opinions. There are lots and lots of opinions going on there.

I feel I should return briefly to the opening statement just to remind you, dear reader, that I am not evil or callous (or maybe I am, but either way): I love my mother.

I do love my mother, what's more I would die without her. But I also can really, really imagine killing her. One day, upon seeing my new haircut, she'll say 'it's nice', in that special way all mothers have that, in just two words, conveys a lifetime of disappointment in you, effortlessly calls to mind your every failure, and makes you want to actually tear your own face off in irritation. In that moment I am afraid that I might kill her, and this would most unfortunately and inevitably lead to a murder-suicide situation, because, as I mentioned, I would die without her. It's a very catch-22 scenario.

Not getting convicted, of course, that part would be fine. Every single person on that jury would have a mother and completely understand that it was an act of self-defence. That in gently smothering her, I was defending my sanity in the face of her chronic interfering and knowing best. I can even imagine a judge, upon hearing that she died at 62, commending me for holding off for so long. For displaying such stoic restraint in the face of repeated maternal barbs about weight gain, the state of my house and my persistent rejection of virtually all of her unsolicited advice.

I love my mother. I really do.

I didn't love her when she gave me a public roasting at my wedding, however. She used her five-minute slot during the speeches to thoroughly lambaste me for every petty adolescent misdemeanour and eccentric rebellion, from being caught smoking behind the art rooms to devoutly attending the city-centre Baptist Church for two weeks when I was 16.

The speech soon spiralled into a full-scale character assassination, including the immortal lines: 'When you become a mother, you have such high hopes for your daughter. But from day one Sophie never did anything I wanted her to. She was always so contrary.' She even brought up the fact that I gave up the piano and dropped all but six subjects in my Leaving. At my wedding. I'm genuinely shocked that she didn't bring up the fact that I (in that conniving way that I have, it's always been implied) gave her mastitis back when she was breastfeeding me.

I have mined our turbulent relationship many times for fodder for my newspaper column and, truthfully, it's all just been one long get-back for that speech.

The relationship is just very, very intense. The mother-daughter thing is like a claustrophobic rage-love affair that's capable of hitting the levels of melodrama usually reserved for daytime soap operas or *Wuthering Heights*.

If it sounds like I'm complaining, I am. But I do recognise that we are intrinsically linked – most of the time it feels distinctly as if the umbilical cord was never cut. Himself thinks that our relationship is borderline destructive, such is the intensity of our daily phone calls, emails and texts. Our most basic interaction can degenerate into Pinteresque levels of subtext, emotional sabotage and mind games within minutes.

I often forget that not everyone is so deeply caught up in the lives of their mothers. I'll find myself moaning to the Bitch Herd about, say, a dinner party that Herself is planning. Head in hands, I'll groan about having so much on this week and how I'm not sure if I can handle my mother's dinner party. To which they'll respond, baffled, 'How does that affect you?' These are women who have, to my mind, as reasonable a relationship as any woman can expect to have with her mother. They talk on the phone three times a week and are frequently berated for not losing weight/returning phone calls/being engaged yet. All normal mother behaviour.

My weekly interactions with my mother are considerably more involved (and frustrating). An average day's correspondence could be several texts, two emails and at least one phone call that begins with an irritated 'Hang on, I'll ring you back', from her. To which I respond, 'But you rang me.' By this time she has already hung up.

Countless jobs and tasks go back and forth between us daily: she's collecting my son, I'm reprogramming the DVD player (she believes that all children born after 1980 come preinstalled with the knowledge of how to do this kind of job), and God help me if she gets wind of a trip to IKEA – suddenly I'm picking up 'a few bits' for her (a Billy bookcase, a 10-piece crockery set) and returning eight throw pillows that didn't make the cut.

But back to that dinner party.

Herself is wonderfully entertaining and possesses an inexhaustible curiosity for everyone she meets. This makes her the best company. But she does not plan well. For someone who loves entertaining she appears barely to survive the stress it causes her. The week preceding any dinner party is always punctuated by lengthy harried phone calls during which she flip-flops back and forth on menu choices. She asks me for suggestions but appears to have absolutely no intention of taking me up on any of them. Finally, she will decide to try one of my recipes, but always with a bizarre, grudging air about it as if she's doing *me* a favour.

From then on my week will be dominated with phone calls about the lamb. Rants about the price of the lamb. Rants about the difficulty of procuring fenugreek in a Tesco Express. Rant-debates about buying pre-blanched almonds versus home-blanching. Then one fecky ingredient too far and she'll scrap the whole plan and revert to one of her regular dishes in the repertoire. Admittedly, they are very good. Her Italian braised beef would probably make it onto the aforementioned 18-course tasting menu.

On the appointed day I often come over to help her. But an extension of my control-freakery is that I can barely stand to even get involved. I like total control, and inheriting someone else's mess does not appeal. She is also the very worst type of multi-tasker, the type that thinks they are very good at multi-tasking but in fact leave a trail of chaos and unfinished jobs in their wake.

She veers wildly between chopping the basil, agonising over the instructions on a bag of microwave vegetables, asking me over and over whether I think the meat should go in yet (she is always dying to put the meat in – as a nervous cook she tends to cook the absolute shite out of meat) and putting on her lipstick. This kind of high-octane, hyperactive approach to, well, everything, totally exhausts me. I used to wonder why she put herself through it. Until I realised that she completely thrives on the stress. It gets her blood up and fuels her incredible appetite for socialising. She is the most gracious and fun host but beyond that she really loves to give everyone a good time.

Being Herself's only child has loomed large in the landscape of my life, though I accept that being the daughter of virtually any mother is tough going. Sometimes I wonder if it's just that we are kind of incompatible as mother and daughter. So much of what I do (or really DON'T do) drives her demented. And, from my perspective, I feel so much of her micro-managing is borderline psychotic. Take, for example, her inordinate interest, nay obsession, with my laundry. Why won't I separate whites from coloureds? Why won't I use a colour catcher? Why can I not grasp the apparently essential separation of delicate whites from non-delicate whites? And why do I insist on using a drying rack? This last one could well be the key to our entire dysfunction. She blames absolutely everything that's wrong with my life on the drying rack. Apparently the drying rack is getting me down. If I say I'm not feeling well, I'm a bit queasy, she'll say emphatically: 'Well, how could you be feeling well, with that thing around?' indicating the drying rack in the corner. If I'm struggling with work, 'It's no wonder, with that drying rack getting in on your head space.' Drying Rack is like the adult equivalent of the bad influence friend during our teenage years. It's all born out of love, I guess, even if it is a mildly suffocating love. And any time this asphyxiating love is withdrawn I do kind of fall to pieces. I can't stand to fight with her and fighting with her is not

like fighting with an ordinary friend, because when fighting with your mother, it's important to remember that it's always your fault. Always. This is how our fights go:

Me: We're doing Kris Kindle with the in-laws this year and everyone is asking for a specific gift, so everyone gets something they want.
Herself: Good idea, what have you asked for?
Me: I've asked for a pair of really, really nice slippers, for a bit of luxury.
Herself: That's a shit present. Why have you asked for that?
Me: Because it's not something that I'd ever buy for myself, and it's what I want.
Herself: If I were you now I'd ask for …
Me: Can you just listen to yourself for one minute? Are you seriously about to start micro-managing my choice in Secret Santa gift?
Herself: Fine. FINE. I'll never offer my opinion on anything ever again.

At this point she will either not speak to me for several days and answer the phone curtly in a special voice she uses when she's pissed off (the best adjective for it would have to be 'tight'). Or she will go on to her extended fight speech:

Herself: 'I'm only trying to help you, but I don't know why I bother, you never listen to a single thing I suggest. But that's it, from now on you can live your own life [I am 30 years old, by the way – I think it's fairly reasonable to want to live one's own life at 30], I'm not going to say a word. I won't give you an opinion on anything ever again [this last bit is definitely a lie].' Then the no talking commences and I invariably become – the only word for it is – heartsick. Himself has to tolerate me flopping around the house sighing and moping. During these times I'd give anything for one of her pesky random requests. Who's putting together her IKEA furniture and changing her light bulbs?, I wonder. Who is she ringing for a chat while stuck in traffic?

(No joke, she does this.) Who will she ask to come over and photograph all of her used furniture and household items, then upload the pictures to DoneDeal and manage the sale and delivery of each item?

Our reunions are usually more grudging than jubilant. Fact is, we need each other, in many ways more than the average mother and daughter need each other – we are what's left of each other's family. Anyway, we are each probably a bit too jaded to make overt proclamations of the 'I love you, you're my best friend' kind. After every fight we come back together to embark once more on our unending ballet of passionate irritation, menial tasks and generalised bitching – nothing changes and no one 'grows', and that is the way we like it.

And fuck it, I love her, she's my best friend.

Also, she makes the best meringues in the world. I know that she would want to me to put that in. Her meringues have been perfected and tweaked more than the equations NASA engineers use to land spaceships on the moon. Herself and her meringues are powerfully, metaphysically linked. A (rare) bad batch will throw her out of orbit. Her outlook will take on a vaguely nihilistic slant and she will start to deeply question her meringue-making abilities. She'll bring it up in conversation from time to time until her next batch is made. A return to form always wipes the slate clean, but until then she will ruminate. I am not the biggest fan of meringues. Not, I hastily add, her meringues particularly, just meringues in general. She, however, takes my lack of enthusiasm as a direct rejection of her. See, Pinter would've had a field day with us.

CHOCOLATE AND ORANGE BREAD-AND-BUTTER PUDDING

Bread-and-butter pudding is one of the first desserts that Herself ever taught me to make. Herself has a sweet tooth that is so strong and dominating it practically holds her hostage in life. In all other things she is admirably moderate and abstemious but when it comes to dessert she is completely powerless. Her delight in sweet things is kind of childlike and most endearing, and this variation on the traditional bread-and-butter pudding is her favourite of everything I make. Any bread can be substituted for the brioche, or even leftover croissant (if there is ever such a thing). This pudding can be reheated in the oven. **Serves 6–8**

- 1 orange
- butter, for greasing, and for buttering the brioche
- 1 small brioche loaf, about 450g, cut into slices
- 4 eggs
- 400ml cream
- 6 tablespoons caster sugar
- 1 teaspoon ground cinnamon
- 150g plain chocolate chips
- crème fraîche, to serve

Place the unpeeled orange in a saucepan, cover it with boiling water and simmer for about an hour, topping up the water if necessary. The orange should be tender. Remove from the pan and set aside until needed. This can be done the night before.

Preheat the oven to 180°C/Gas 4. Generously grease a 30 x 20-cm baking dish, then butter both sides of each slice of brioche. Put the eggs, cream, 5 tablespoons of the sugar, the cinnamon and the entire orange into a food processor and blitz until smooth.

Arrange a layer of overlapping brioche slices in the prepared dish, sprinkle over half the chocolate chips, tucking some between the slices, and pour over half the egg mixture. Arrange the remaining brioche slices on top, sprinkle with the remaining chocolate chips and pour over more of the egg mix.

Leave to stand until the brioche has absorbed the egg mixture, then sprinkle with the remaining sugar and place in the middle of the preheated oven (on a baking tray in case of overflow). Bake for about 35 minutes. The loaf will puff up and the top should have a nice golden crust to it, while the middle will be set but still moist.

Serve warm with a dollop of crème fraîche.

MERINGUE ROULADE

I've spoken before about Herself's exceptional meringues and she even
generously offered to give me her recipe to include in this book but I, never
one to pass up the opportunity to annoy her, decided to eschew her meringues
for Himself's famous hazelnut meringue roulade. Tasty and infinitely more
showboaty. And now I can finally call it quits over that speech she gave at my
wedding.

Herself endlessly debates the merits of adding the sugar a teaspoon at a time
versus adding it in a slow, steady trickle. She gets very irritated when I claim to
throw it all in and still get perfect meringues. **Serves 12**

- rapeseed oil, for brushing
- 5 egg whites
- 275g caster sugar
- 1 teaspoon cornflour
- 100g hazelnuts, toasted and
  chopped
- 1 teaspoon icing sugar (optional)
- 300ml whipping cream
- 250g fresh strawberries and
  blackberries, sliced

Preheat the oven to 200°C/Gas 6. Line a 35 x
25-cm baking tray with baking paper and brush
with a little oil. Line a board with baking paper.

Put the egg whites into a clean, grease-free
bowl and whisk with a hand-held electric
mixer until they hold stiff peaks. Add the caster
sugar and beat until the mixture is thick and
glossy. Beat in the cornflour, ensuring it is well
combined.

My trick for testing when the mixture is beaten
enough is to scoop up a little dollop with one
index finger. Hold your hands up, palms facing,
and press your index fingertips together, then
draw them apart. When it's ready, the mixture
should come to a point straight out from your
finger and not droop. Stir in the hazelnuts.

Spread the mixture evenly on the prepared
tray. Bake in the preheated oven for 8 minutes,

then reduce the oven temperature to 160°C/
Gas 3 and bake for a further 15 minutes until
it is puffed up with a firm crust. Leave to cool
on the tray for 15 minutes, then gently turn
out upside-down onto the prepared board and
carefully remove the backing paper from the
meringue. Leave to cool completely.

Just before serving, sift the icing sugar, if using,
into the cream and whip until it holds soft peaks.
Cover two-thirds of the meringue with two-thirds
of the cream, reserving the remainder for the
top. Gently roll the roulade along the long edge,
using the paper underneath to roll it and prevent
it cracking too much. Spread the remaining
cream over the roulade and arrange the sliced
berries on top. Cut into 12 slices and serve.

CHICKEN AND MANGO SALAD

This is Herself's take on Thai Larb Gai and makes a great light summer supper. I always feel very virtuous having salad for dinner; even just calling dinner supper makes me feel lighter and more streamlined, thus paving the way for my after-'supper' gorging, which is a sight to behold. (See my Bounty truffles on page 73 for further details.) **Serves 2 as a light supper**

- 1 tablespoon sesame oil
- 2 skinless chicken breasts, finely chopped, or 300g fresh chicken mince
- pinch of salt
- 1 tablespoon grated fresh ginger
- 1 garlic clove, grated
- juice of 1 lime
- 1 tablespoon rice wine vinegar
- pinch of dried chilli flakes
- 4 spring onions, finely sliced
- 2 tablespoons chopped fresh coriander
- 2 tablespoons chopped fresh mint
- 2 tablespoons chopped fresh basil
- 2 generous handfuls crunchy salad leaves
- 1 mango, peeled and chopped
- lime wedges, to serve

Heat the oil in a frying pan over a medium–high heat and add the chicken, salt, ginger and garlic, then stir-fry until the chicken is cooked through. Remove the pan from the heat and stir in the lime juice, vinegar, chilli flakes, spring onions, coriander, mint and basil.

Divide the salad leaves and mango between two bowls and pour over the warm chicken mixture. Serve with the lime wedges.

CHAPTER 20

Why going mad was the best thing that ever happened to me

In which I reflect on how despite many YEARS IN THE WILDERNESS of medication, relapse and general plot-losing, if I went back in time I would still take that little pill.

SO THE TITLE OF THIS CHAPTER MAY BE SOMETHING OF AN OVERSTATEMENT, but still, despite the difficult period in my early 20s, I would never take it back. If I could wind back every day of my life since then to that moment right before I took that tiny pill, would I still take it? I would. It's taken me 10 years to feel that way, but the truth is I have to take it, in order to get me back to the here and now. I don't expect anyone in the throes of anguish and mental illness to feel the same. If you are reading this on a locked ward, or lying in a bed that you cannot get out of, then you are maybe thinking that what happened to me was different from what's happening to you, that perhaps it was milder or it was easier for me to wrest my mind back from my illness. It was, or it wasn't, there's no way to tell. And certainly there's no point in comparing. What's happening to each of us is worse because it's happening to us.

One of my favourite phrases is 'Other people's pain is easy to bear'. I don't see it as a callous thing. I just think that each and every person has an abyss inside them and, frankly, it's work to be human and stay sane. To not dwell on the negatives. Trying to describe a mental illness is difficult – no one description will represent everyone. Even for the purpose of writing this book I found it hard to go back to my madness and to pick it up, to handle it, without a slight fear that I would be invaded again. Andrew asked me to describe it to him and this is what I came up with:

> My madness feels like I am standing at the very edge of a cliff, but with my back to the precipice. I am facing inland towards safety and family and friends and breakfast and TV and life, but behind me, clawing at my back, is a huge black ocean. This ocean is as thick as oil and it rears up and down, wild and furious, and I am terrified that it will pull me in. Also, it is strangely nearly irresistible, and I don't know why that is. In every moment, as I face the land

and smile and eat and do things, the madness roars at my back. I can never not feel it. Only a tiny, slight, minuscule shift in my body and I'll be sucked back and down and under. And beneath that roiling surface? It is as terrifying and as empty as Space. I know because I went under for a while. I stared out from the sockets of my eyes and wore my face like a mask. And I tried, I really tried to act normal, but inside my body was full up with the black frightful ocean and it was choking me, like I was drowning from the inside.

And once your brain betrays you like this, it's hard to ever trust yourself again. It's like a beloved pet that one day lashes out and you realise forever what that animal is capable of. Even as you recover and the years go by and there are more and more days of normal, boring, unremarkable, wonder strung together like small misshapen pearls. And even as much as we remind ourselves of the tragedies of others – we don't have cancer and our limbs are intact – frankly this kind of rationale is fairly pointless in the face of mental illness. It's about as good as saying of my father, at least he has the use of his legs! It's not much good is it? That's the bloody pisser of mental illness – we are held hostage by our brainsick brains. And, sadly for many, diseases of the brain come off as vaguely self-indulgent, not least in a scenario like mine where I kind of brought it on myself. 'Other people's pain is easy to bear.'

But back to that little pill.

Yes, I would still take it, because from where I stand now I don't know what would have become of me had I not. Perhaps the other outcome would've been far, far worse. And now I understand that those difficult years had to happen. I don't think they made me a better person or anything, but they did make me in some way. They certainly steered my life in an unexpected direction. Before I became unwell I don't think I even owned a pair of runners. After I started to feel better little by little, I didn't know what I should really spend my time doing. I had spent a good chunk of my life drinking, smoking weed, hungover and making art. Since I didn't really know what I wanted to be doing any more I tried out lots of things. I wanted to live in tents and walk in the mountains and snowboard and ski and cook and eat and read and I spent my 20s doing those things. For the most part, I lived quite deliberately and carefully during those years. I minded myself, because I had to. I was prone to setbacks that, while they were happening, felt never-ending. And I was still on the Lexapro for a few years. As Himself and I moved from job to job and country to country, I felt good in our slightly rootless existence, good about never planning anything or committing to anything more fixed than where we would live for the next few months. This was the best I could do at the time. Plans, however pleasant they might have been, scared me. My main aim was to keep on moving, keep busy and keep the thoughts at bay.

When we moved back to Ireland and wound up expecting a surprise baby, for the first time in years I was wrenched out of my careful self-containment. Here, suddenly, was a little being who wouldn't understand if I was feeling brainsick or unable to deal with the world. And a little being that was going to need quite a lot of commitment and effort on my part. It was time to re-engage. Everything since madness had up until that point felt quite like a long, rambling life tangent that I suppose I presumed I would claw my way back from at some stage. I suspect that even my on-paper successful friends who didn't drop out of life for the best part of a decade can feel like this from time to time. I probably shouldn't put everything down to the waxing and waning of madness, as all our lives are these cycles of good and bad times. The trick is knowing the good times, I guess, recognising those unremarkable pearls as we drag ourselves through the days of mild drudgery, never realising that it is this very drudgery that we will long for after the ocean takes us. In fact, currently I'm writing these words from a place of mild drudgery. It is 7.00 pm and the rain is doing one of those special, quintessentially Irish mist-blankets that rain in this country is so good at. The kind of half-assed rain that manages to get one wetter than if it was just a good old downpour. Nick Drake is singing 'Time Has Told Me', which is so apt. I swear I'm not making it up. Yer Man is desperately trying to thwart my typing with his cars and Himself is making some kind of hell-concoction with chickpeas, bread and limp kale in the kitchen. This is a good day.

And this is why I think this story wanted telling, because back when I thought I was going to kill my family, or at the very least commit suicide, I never thought that I would have a good day again. During that time all I wanted was evidence that you could feel this weird and shit and fucked up and still come through it. So I thought it was worth talking about it. It took me a good while to start feeling able to talk about it without feeling scared and instantly nauseous. And another while before I could fully admit why it happened. Or at least what the trigger was. I don't know if I fully believe that drugs and drugs alone were the complete why of the thing – one of my doctors once told me that I may have had it in me all along. And a good thing to remember is that there's usually a lot of whys about this type of thing. I do think that for me the drugs added an extra layer to the base layer of mental health stigma. I think I took longer to get help when I was seriously in need, simply because I didn't want to admit that I had brought it on myself.

When we had my dad admitted to the wildly unsuitable psychiatric ward after he had attacked my mother, it was my first time back in a psychiatric institution since my early 20s. I got to know the people on the ward, who were unfailingly kind to my dad. They were clearly struggling so much in their own lives, but every time I went there to walk laps of the atrium with Kev, I would be told again and again by his ward-mates what a gentle man he was. And how young he was, and what a shame it was – by people who were in every bit as bad a way as him.

Kev spent in all about four months on that ward. In that time he was as lucid as he was ever going to be again. Which is to say, not very. At times he was wild and skittish, talking about cats that weren't there, but still responding, if a little haphazardly, to questions we asked him. Other days he was verging on catatonic. On these days I felt the best mode of communication was head rubs and listening to music in his room. At home I was weaning my son onto real food and at the hospital I was feeding my dad his dinner from a spoon. At times I'd catch myself making the baby feeding noises – 'nom noms' – to Kev instead of the baby. It was a bit disorienting. Then one day I spied a stack of adult nappies in his bedside locker and I went back to my car in the car park and bawled for a few minutes. Now I think about Nappy Day as potentially part of my own future (a bit like Botox Day or Asking For the Music To Be Turned Down in a Restaurant Day) and vow that I will never let it get to that point.

Being back in that ward reminded me so much of the counsellors and the psychiatrists and the Styrofoam cups of milky tea and the dry mouth and the taste of brainsick. I wondered if the other people there would get through their illnesses. And I met a boy I used to know, Jake. He had gone so deep under that he barely seemed to acknowledge that he was in a hospital. And he certainly didn't remember me or seem to see me. He walked around very slowly as though the floor was soft and squishy, and he made gestures to people who weren't there.

I gave his dad a lift home one night. We didn't say that much about our respective patients. I told him that I had known Jake as a teenager in school, where he had been a stand-out character for his creativity and virtually unheard-of (in a sea of teenagers) emotional intelligence. His dad told me snippets about the intervening years. Drugs. Mania. Diagnosis. Months at home doing well and weeks spent back under, inside the hospital. The waxing and waning. He was not expansive on the subject and I didn't pry. And anyway the details were not necessary;

the story was familiar to me. As perhaps it is to you. He smiled when he spoke of his son and I dropped him off. I went home and looked at my own son and thought of Jake and his father and thought: 'That is the greatest pain in the world.'

A few weeks later, as Kev and I did our lap, Jake and his dad came towards us, each smiling slightly. They are incredibly alike side by side. And so are Kev and I, I've always been told (to my chagrin, I might add – what woman wants to look like a middle-aged man, after all?). Later, I see them, heads bent together, apparently talking, which is more engaged than I'd ever seen Jake. Jake's father and I fall into step as we are leaving. 'Today,' he says, 'was a good day.'

CHICKEN-FRIED CAULIFLOWER RICE

Having spent the best part of 10 years eating, writing about eating and cooking, you'd think I'd lose the love at some point, but no, eating is my life's work. And I still get a kick out of gloatingly sending the Bitch Herd pictures of deep-fried Mars bars (see page 112), captioned 'tough day at the office'. I don't think I am overstating things in the slightest when I say that cooking saved my life. My first day working in a kitchen my hands shook from the medication I was on, my mouth was perennially dry and I was having a hard time concentrating on my colleagues' instructions because there was a constant ringing in my ears. I had spent months trying to regain some kind of control in my life. I was afraid to be idle even for a second in case the howling, uncontrollable thoughts would return, maybe this time with no let-up. Here, in a claustrophobic, loud, clattering kitchen, nearly 20,000 kilometres from home, was at last something that felt like refuge. I could pick up this knife and follow orders and think of nothing but the simple act of applying heat to matter. If I could just stay in the moment and think only of the task at hand, I would be safe. And I was safe. And then, gradually, I was happy.

Learning to cook in a Kiwi kitchen 10 years ago was an eye-opener for me at a time when tastes in Ireland were somewhat less evolved than they are today. In New Zealand fusion is not so much a trend as an unconscious underlying element to much of their food, drawing as it does from Asia, Europe and Polynesia. This has definitely informed my tastes ever since, as these recipes illustrate.

The recent trend for vegetables masquerading as carbs really suits me. The potato/rice/pasta component of any meal wouldn't be my highest priority on a plate – I'm more of a meat/sauce/cheese girl. I also find rice and pasta incredibly filling and resent the fact that after a plate of these I'm in no state for the meat/cheese/dessert portion of the evening. This chicken-fried rice has hoodwinked many a rice devotee, my own mother included. People genuinely don't notice that it's not rice mainly because it's pretty damn delicious. And healthy – bonus.

Serves 2 as a main or 4 as a side

- *2 skinless chicken breasts, each sliced into 5 strips*
- *2 tablespoons soy sauce, plus extra for frying*
- *2 tablespoons rice wine vinegar*
- *1 tablespoon wholegrain mustard*
- *1 tablespoon clear honey*
- *1 tablespoon sweet chilli sauce*
- *1 tablespoon Chinese five-spice powder*
- *2 tablespoons chopped fresh ginger*
- *1 garlic clove, finely sliced*
- *2 carrots, finely diced*
- *80g frozen peas*
- *4 spring onions, finely sliced*
- *2 eggs, beaten*
- *1 large head of cauliflower, florets grated*
- *sunflower oil, for frying*
- *small bunch of fresh coriander*

Preheat the oven to 180°C/Gas 4. Place the chicken strips in a 20-cm square baking tray. Add the soy sauce, vinegar, mustard, honey, sweet chilli sauce and five-spice powder, along with the ginger and garlic. Mix to combine, coating the chicken well.

Cook in the preheated oven for 20 minutes, or until the chicken is cooked through.

Arrange the vegetables on individual plates within easy reach of the hob.

Use two forks to pull the chicken apart, leaving it in what remains of the marinade – this gives the meat loads of flavour and keeps it nice and moist.

Heat a little oil in a large non-stick frying pan over a high heat and add the carrots. Stir-fry for 1–2 minutes to soften slightly, then add the peas, spring onions and eggs. Using a spatula, quickly scramble the eggs among the vegetables. Throw in the chicken, the remaining marinade and the cauliflower and stir-fry, adding a little more soy sauce. Ensure that everything is well combined, then divide between bowls, top with the coriander and serve.

SALMON MINI-BURGERS WITH PICKLED BEETROOT AND GINGER AND NOODLE SALAD

Himself has long held out in his War Against Fish and I find billing it as burgers is the best way to get him to eat it. You'll need to make the pickle well ahead of time! **Makes 4 mini-burgers (serves 2)**

- 250g salmon fillets, skinned, boned and chopped
- 2 spring onions, finely chopped
- 1 generous teaspoon wasabi paste, plus extra to serve
- 3 tablespoons black sesame seeds, toasted
- 20g plain flour
- 1 tablespoon rapeseed oil
- salt and freshly ground black pepper

Pickled ginger and beetroot

- 150ml rice wine vinegar
- 150ml water
- 80g sugar
- 1 tablespoon salt
- 325g raw beetroot, mixed red and golden, peeled and sliced into wafer-thin rounds
- 50g fresh ginger, peeled and sliced into wafer-thin rounds

To serve

- 120g dried fine egg noodles or vermicelli noodles, cooked according to the packet instructions and rinsed in cold water
- 1 tablespoon sesame oil
- 1 grapefruit
- 35g salted peanuts
- small handful of mixed fresh basil, mint and coriander, finely chopped
- ½ avocado, sliced

First, make the pickled ginger and beetroot. Combine the vinegar, water, sugar and salt in a bowl and add the beetroot and ginger. Leave to stand for at least 4 hours. Transfer to a mason jar and store for up to 1 month.

Remove any small bones from the salmon and chop. In a bowl, mix the salmon, spring onions, wasabi paste, sesame seeds and flour and season with salt and pepper. Shape into 8 mini patties, then chill in the fridge for 30 minutes.

Heat the rapeseed oil in a frying pan over a medium–high heat, add the burgers and fry for 3–5 minutes on each side, or until they are golden and cooked through.

To serve, toss the cooled noodles in the sesame oil. Peel the grapefruit and cut into bite-sized slices, removing any pips, and add these to the noodles along with the peanuts and the chopped herbs. Combine well and divide between two bowls. Top with the avocado slices, salmon burgers and some pickle.

LAMB BURGERS AND SWEET POTATO WEDGES WITH BEETROOT TOPPING

Himself can be a bit of a snob about certain things food-related. He thinks peanut butter is 'too American' and that sweetcorn is 'tacky'. When it comes to burgers he is a complete purist and thinks that anything beyond a simple understated beef burger of good meat with minimal accompaniments is too 'try hard'. Suffice to say, my burger is not understated. It is try hard. It is the Donatella Versace of hamburgers.

Still, I happen to think it is rather good and, for once, there's not much argument out of Himself. Make sure you're hungry for this mammoth feast. It's hard to believe, but I don't think I'd ever met a sweet potato, or kumara as the Kiwis call them, until I got to New Zealand. It was the start of a great love affair.

Serves 5

Lamb burgers

- *1 tablespoon olive oil*
- *1 red onion, finely chopped*
- *3 garlic cloves, crushed*
- *2 tablespoons fresh rosemary, finely chopped*
- *1 tablespoon juniper berries, crushed*
- *1 tablespoon smoked paprika*
- *1 tablespoon ground cumin*
- *500g fresh lamb mince*
- *75g porridge oats*
- *1 egg*
- *1 teaspoon salt*

Sweet potato wedges

- *6–8 sweet potatoes (about 1.2kg)*
- *4–6 tablespoons olive oil*
- *2 tablespoons paprika*
- *salt and freshly ground black pepper*

Beetroot topping

- *2 large cooked beetroot*
- *100g Greek-style yogurt*
- *1 teaspoon honey*
- *10 mint leaves*
- *10 walnuts*
- *freshly ground black pepper*

To serve

- *toasted pitta bread*
- *salad leaves*
- *feta cheese or blue cheese*
- *crème fraîche*

To make the sweet potato wedges, preheat the oven to 210°C/Gas 7. Cut the sweet potatoes into wedges and toss them in the oil, paprika, and salt and pepper. Arrange them on a baking tray in a single layer, without overcrowding the tray, and bake in the preheated oven for 45 minutes or until cooked through and nicely charred.

Meanwhile, make the burgers. Heat the oil in a frying pan over a low heat and add the onion, garlic, rosemary, juniper berries, paprika and cumin. Cook until the onions have softened to a paste-like consistency, adding a dash of water if the mixture is too dry, and set aside.

Put the lamb into a bowl with the oats, egg and salt and mix together with your hands. Add the onion mixture, mix well and shape into 5 good-sized patties. Chill the burgers in the fridge while you make the topping.

Put all the ingredients for the beetroot topping into a food processor and blend until smooth. The consistency should be roughly that of hummus.

Pan-fry or grill the burgers for about 5–8 minutes on each side, then transfer to the oven for about 5 minutes, or until cooked through. Serve in toasted pitta bread with salad leaves, cheese and the beetroot topping, with the sweet potato wedges and a dollop of crème fraîche on the side.

ULTIMATE BEST (FLOURLESS) CHOCOLATE CAKE EVER

Himself originally wrangled the recipe from a naïve Danish pastry chef who happened across his path during his tenure in another Kiwi kitchen; she had no idea of the kind of power she possessed with this cake recipe. He has always hinted that some despicable misdeed on his part was needed to get it but I have never probed too deeply, lest I discover that it was attained through some kind of actual probing, and could therefore never enjoy the chocolate cake again.

This cake is kind of a torte as it uses ground almonds instead of flour and beaten egg whites instead of a raising agent. Himself (the self-appointed oracle on all things baking-related in our house) always offers sage advice whenever I embark on a cake. He says things like 'Just like dogs, cakes can smell fear', and 'Don't wear your neuroses on your sleeve when baking'. Helpful. **You will get 16–20 reasonable-sized slices from this (depending on greed levels).**

- *250g butter*
- *250g plain chocolate*
- *250g caster sugar*
- *8 egg yolks*
- *250g ground almonds*
- *8 egg whites*
- *about 1 tablespoon lemon juice*
- *whipped cream, squashed fresh berries and cocoa to serve*

Preheat the oven to 150°C/Gas 2. Line a 25-cm round springform or loose-based cake tin with baking paper.

Place the butter and the chocolate in a saucepan and heat over a low heat, stirring, until melted. Remove from the heat and leave to cool.

Using a hand-held electric mixer and the whisk attachments, beat the sugar and egg yolks together until pale and doubled in volume. Add the chocolate mixture and mix well to combine. Stir in the ground almonds. Put the egg whites into a clean, grease-free bowl with the lemon juice and whisk until they hold soft peaks.

Add about a quarter of the egg white to the chocolate mixture to loosen it a bit, then carefully fold through the remaining egg white. The trick is to combine the chocolate mixture and the whisked egg whites thoroughly but to also retain the airiness. Basically, don't beat the crap out of it, as Himself always patiently instructs.

Carefully pour the batter into the prepared tin and bake in the middle of the oven for 1 hour–1 hour 15 minutes. Try to ignore the temptation to open the door and poke at it, as I always want to do.

After 1 hour, gently insert a skewer into the centre of the cake. The cake is ready when the skewer comes out almost clean. Remove from the oven and leave in the tin to cool completely, then unclip and remove the springform.

Serve with whipped cream with a few squashed berries folded through it and dust with a little cocoa.

ACKNOWLEDGEMENTS

Writing acknowledgements is the closest I will ever come to a thrilling Oscars-style speech, so I am going to seriously revel in this unique opportunity to laud the anointed ones among my acquaintances and subtly damn the bastards with my gently crushing omission. Here we go …

First up, a huge thanks to everyone who worked on *Recipes for a Nervous Breakdown*. At Gill Books, so much gratitude to Teresa Daly (for believing in the book and convincing others to do likewise), Nicki Howard (who contributed, among many other things, to the book's title), Deirdre Nolan (who helped to conceive the idea) and Sarah Liddy (who took care of the gestation). To Fiona Biggs and Catherine Gough for their careful editing. To the gang who made the book look so damn fine: Jette Virdi styled the absolute shit out of these beautiful pictures taken by Leo Byrne, and Graham Thew managed to bring the various disparate elements together to create a cookbook memoir like no other. I am also forever grateful to Aoife Coghlan, my kitchen bitch partner in crime, who spent five days with me in a 6ft by 4ft kitchen and didn't kill me.

To Susan Jane White, who is my neighbour in *Life* magazine and who generously suggested me to Gill Books as a person who could perhaps make a book. I definitely owe the existence of *Recipes for a Nervous Breakdown* to her. I want to thank Emily Hourican, who generously explained to me the ins and outs of dealing with big, evil publishing overlords and kindly read this book and offered excellent advice.

To Brendan O'Connor, my editor at *Life* magazine. I would definitely never have found out I wanted to write things without Brendan's encouragement and belief in me. He also taught me about fucking about – basically not to do it. He rules my life with equal measures benevolence and (admittedly occasionally necessary) tyranny. He is referred to in my house only as 'B', which I think he would enjoy as it communicates just how feared and revered he is in the White household. Thank you, B.

Thank you to the book club bitches for the wine and chats and the all-important 'minutes'. And to Lia Hynes and Aidan Lawlor, the Bob and Carol to our Alice and Ted, if that's not too creepy a reference – I look forward to welcoming Sarah as a daughter-in-law one day. To Sarah Caden, thank you for patiently answering my extremely basic parenting queries and assembling all the Ikea furniture at number 89 so I don't have to.

I would like to thank my family at HerFamily.ie and Maximum Media, especially Sive O'Brien, Katie Mythen, Sharyn Hayden, Trine Jensen and Rebecca McKnight, who all suffered by my side during my most recent gestation and supplied me with a lot of corn snacks.

I would like to thank The Bitch Herd, most especially Jen O'Dwyer, Jess Pierce and Rebecca Coll, who have allowed me to mine our lives together for many a column. These women basically raised me and played no small part in saving me from serial teenage humiliation. Thank you, bitches, you're the best bitches a girl could ask for.

A huge debt of gratitude is owed to my in-laws, especially my mother- and father-in-law, Vivianne and David White, who tolerate my serial over-truthing and bad-mouthing their son in my weekly column, 'The Domestic'.

I am rather short on siblings but the Harris girls are the best pseudo-sisters I could ever have: Anne, Nancy and Connie are always loving, encouraging and willing recipients of head rubs.

To my dad, Kevin Linehan, who will never read this but whom I would like to thank all the same. There is no better father. I do think of you every day. I miss what a soothing presence you were in all our lives. And thanks for leaving me with a hundred ways to remember you happily every day.

I will never finish being grateful to my mother, Mary O'Sullivan. She is the most fun-loving, passionate, interesting woman I know. There are certain downsides to having your own mother as your best friend (see Chapter 19), but there's also no one else whose sense of humour is quite so evil. She has given me everything; even the basic fact of allowing this book to be published is a testament to her generosity of spirit, being that it's an occasionally damning indictment of her parenting abilities.

To Seb, aka Himself, aka The Man, aka my husband, who by some miracle wanted to be around me and still does. Seriously, thank you. I am 87 per cent confident that we're on to a winner here. And, thanks to you, the babies are very beautiful.

INDEX